SABRE JET ACE

BY CHARLES COOMBS
ILLUSTRATED BY ROD RUTH

PURPLE HOUSE PRESS　KENTUCKY

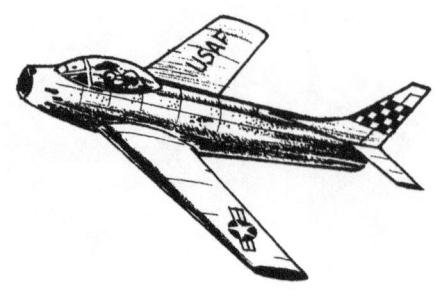

Published by
Purple House Press
PO Box 787
Cynthiana, Kentucky 41031

Classic Books for Kids and Young Adults
purplehousepress.com

Written in 1959 by Charles Coombs
Copyright © 2024 by Purple House Press
All rights reserved

Photo credits: front cover copyright © 2022 by Mike Killian,
back cover US Air Force, Suwon Air Base, Korea, May 18, 1953

The F-86F on the cover did fly in the US Air Force beginning in 1952. It is owned and piloted by Doug Matthews, who painstakingly restored it with Classic Fighters of America, and painted it to honor Captain Joseph McConnell Jr.'s last F-86F.

ISBN 9798888180648 Paperback
ISBN 9798888180655 Hardcover

CONTENTS

From Model Planes to Army Medic

1.	EYES OF AN EAGLE	1
2.	TOO YOUNG FOR THE AIR CORPS	10
3.	THE OLD ONE-TWO	16
4.	PILLS, TAGS, AND BAGS OF FLOUR	27
5.	PEARL HARBOR	37

Wings

6.	AIR CADET	44
7.	FLYING SCHOOL	54
8.	THE LONG HOP	64
9.	CREW OF THE *SCREAMING EAGLE*	73
10.	BANDITS AROUND THE CLOCK	82
11.	BOMBS AWAY!	92

Sizzling Jets

12.	PILOT WINGS	101
13.	THE TIGER ROARS	114
14.	TEN FEET TALL	124
15.	KOREA	132

Sabres Over Korea

16.	MIG ALLEY	141
17.	FLIGHT LEADER	154
18.	FIRST STAR	162
19.	JET ACE	171
20.	SPECIAL MISSION	181
21.	BAIL OUT	188
22.	BRAVE MEN AND BULLETS	194
23.	LAST FLIGHT	204

EYES OF AN EAGLE
CHAPTER 1

THE HUM OF A SMALL AIRPLANE sounded across the park of a New Hampshire town. The hum of its engine grew louder as it flew around and around.

All at once the plane began to wobble. The wing tipped too far to one side. Young Joseph McConnell, Jr. fought with the controls to right, the plane. Sweat rolled down his tanned face and into his dark eyes.

He heard his friend Steve call to him, "Hey, Mac! What's the matter?"

There was no time to answer. Suddenly the plane nosed down sharply. The tip of one wing almost hit a tall tree in the park.

"Pull her up, Mac!" The shout rang out again. "Pull her up!"

Mac tugged at the control stick. But he could not pull the plane out of the dive. He jerked at the controls again. Hard. A wire snapped.

1

Now, with a broken control stick, there was no way for Mac to keep his plane in the air. As it dived straight toward the ground, he braced himself and waited.

Crash!

Pieces of the plane flew everywhere. Mac ducked as the small engine whizzed past him. Pieces of wood, parts of the wing, bits of metal fell around him. Then everything was quiet.

"Hey, Mac," Steve was calling to him again. "Are you hurt?"

Mac shook his head and turned to his friend, Steve Davis. He saw the worry in Steve's blue eyes, and grinned.

"No. I'm not hurt," he answered. "Who gets hurt flying a model airplane?"

Steve took off his thick horn-rimmed glasses and rubbed his eyes. "When she crashed, the engine broke loose and went flying through the air like a bullet."

"I saw it just in time to duck," Mac said.

"Lucky for you. It might have taken off the top of your head."

Mac laughed. He tugged at his dark hair. "See. Still in one piece. But I can't say the same for our model airplane."

He looked at the broken pieces that were scattered over the ground.

"It's a wreck, all right," Steve agreed. "And we paid a lot just for that engine alone, Mac."

"Don't I know it! Remember how hard we worked cutting grass to earn the money?"

Mac leaned down and picked up a piece of the broken wing. He looked at it for a second, then tossed it away.

"What happened?" Steve asked.

Mac held up the short piece of the stick he still had in his hand. Only minutes before it had been the control stick of their model plane. Two thin wires had stretched from each end of the stick to the model. By using these wires—by tipping the stick back and forth—a "pilot" could fly the plane, guiding it from the ground.

Now one of the long control wires was broken. Mac pointed to it and said, "I think I twisted the wires some way or other. Maybe when I tried to make the plane do a loop. Anyway, when it nosed over and started to dive I jerked too hard on the stick. A wire broke. Cr-rr-ash!"

Steve nodded. "Well, there isn't much you can do when a control wire breaks."

"Just wait for the crash."

"We'll put stronger wires on our next model," Steve said. "Let's go home and get started."

Mac looked at his friend. What a pal! Steve might be a little shy. Skinny, too. At times he reminded Mac of an owl, looking out through his thick glasses.

In fact, Mac and Steve were about as much like

each other as black and white or hot and cold. But they were friends. Good friends.

"How about it?" Steve spoke up again. "We still have enough wood left to make another model."

Mac grinned. You couldn't help liking a fellow like Steve. A fellow who wouldn't give up, who wouldn't quit when things went wrong.

"Sure, we could do it," Mac said, "only—"

"What's the matter, Mac?"

"Well, I was thinking we might lay off making another model for a while."

"Lay off? You mean quit?"

Mac didn't like the word. "No, not quit," he answered. "Just do something else."

"Like what?"

Mac didn't answer right away. How could he tell Steve what was on his mind? How could he tell this skinny, shy boy of his new plan?

It would mean the end of their being together. But not the end of being good friends. Distance didn't matter to friends. A friend was a friend if he was right here beside you, or if he was a thousand miles away.

"Do something like what?" Steve asked again, pulling Mac out of his thoughts.

"Well, it's just this," Mac answered. "It's about time

for me to start learning how to fly a real plane, Steve. After all, we can't fly models all our lives."

"All our lives! We're only seventeen."

"You're seventeen." Mac threw back his shoulders. "I'm eighteen, and if I'm ever going to be a pilot, I should get started."

"So that's it," Steve said, nodding his head. "So that's what has been bothering you. Mac, you would make a good pilot. One of the best. But how will you pay for flying lessons? How can you make enough money for that?"

"I've figured out a plan, Steve. And I think it will work."

Mac pointed to some buildings across from the park. "What's that big white building over there?"

"It's the post office," Steve answered. "The Dover Post Office."

"Right you are," Mac said. "And see that sign in front of it? The one that says:

UNCLE SAM NEEDS YOU!
BE A FLIER
JOIN THE ARMY AIR CORPS."

Steve looked at Mac and then at the sign again. "You—you mean you can read it from here!"

Mac wished he had said nothing about being able to read the sign. Both boys loved flying with all their hearts. Both knew that a pilot needed good sharp eyes. Both knew the day would come when Mac would go on alone. For his dream—his one dream—to become a pilot was nothing new.

The two boys were quiet for a while, each busy with his own thoughts.

At last it was Steve who said, "You'll make it. You

have eyes like an eagle. Mac, the eagle! That's what I'll call—"

Mac broke in with a laugh. "Say, that's great! An eagle can fly. And anything that can fly is for me. That's why I'm going to join the Air Corps."

"They'll be lucky to get you."

Mac smiled. What a friend! "Thanks, Steve. Boy, I wish we could go in together."

"With my eyes?" Steve asked. "I haven't a chance, Mac."

"You could be a mechanic or something. You're a whiz at fixing engines. Why not? The more I think of it—"

"I'm only seventeen," Steve reminded. "And besides, I told my folks I'd wait. After all, I haven't finished high school yet like you."

"I forgot. You're right. Wait until you are out of school. I know my folks wouldn't have agreed for me to join until I had graduated."

"Then you have talked it over with them?"

"Sure," Mac answered. "I wouldn't do anything like joining the Air Corps without talking it over with my folks."

"When are you going to enlist?"

An idea came to Mac. "Why not today? Why not right now?"

Steve looked at him. "Boy, you don't take much time to make up your mind."

"No point in holding off."

"I'll miss you," Steve said. "But no matter what happens, I sure wish you the best luck in the world."

Mac swallowed hard. And for some reason he couldn't explain, he kicked at a piece of broken airplane wing lying on the grass.

"Want to come along with me to the post office?" he asked.

Steve shook his head. "No, I'll wait here. And thanks, Mac. Thanks a lot."

"Thanks for what?"

"For being my friend."

"That was easy, pal."

Mac turned away and headed across the park. Behind him he heard Steve blowing his nose. But he didn't look back to see why. He knew.

His own eyes filled a little at the thought of their parting.

TOO YOUNG FOR THE AIR CORPS
CHAPTER 2

MAC CUT ACROSS the park to the Dover Post Office. Running up the steps, he turned and waved to Steve. Then seeing himself in the glass door, he stopped and smoothed down his dark hair.

"Joe McConnell reporting, sir," he said, looking at himself. "Five feet eight inches of flying fighting man. Show me my plane."

He stopped. "Better not try it that way," he told himself. "They'll kick me out on my ear before I even see a plane."

Mac opened the door and went inside. He hurried down a long hall to a sign on a door marked UNITED STATES ARMY. ENLIST HERE.

Since the door was open, Mac threw back his shoulders and walked into the room. The room was a small one. Just big enough to hold a desk, a few chairs lined up along a wall, and a small table.

A soldier, wearing a tan uniform with the three stripes of an army sergeant, was sitting at the desk.

"What can I do for you?" he said, putting down the papers he had been reading. "Want to sign up to be a soldier?"

"I would rather sign up to be a pilot, sir," Mac answered.

The sergeant looked him over carefully. Mac "stood tall," as they say. He hoped it would make him look ready and fit to be a pilot in the Army Air Corps.

"At ease," the sergeant said, smiling. "You will have your fill of standing at attention once you are in the army. So you want to be a pilot—a flying cadet?"

"Yes, sir."

"What's your name?"

"Joseph McConnell, Jr., sir. But everyone calls me Mac."

"How old are you, Mac?"

"Eighteen, sir."

The sergeant shook his head. "Eighteen is too young to sign up for pilot training."

"But, sir, the sign out front says the army needs fliers."

"We do. There's a war going on in Europe, you know. The United States may be in it one of these days. We must be ready. Sure, we need fliers. But we want them to be at least twenty-one years old."

"I can run faster and fight harder than some fellows I know who are twenty-one." Mac stopped, his face red. "Sir, I didn't mean to sound off."

"That's all right. Sure, you're a husky fellow. But can you think better than a twenty-one-year-old?"

Mac listened quietly as the sergeant went on. "It

takes brains to fly a plane, boy. Sure, you need to be strong and quick with your muscles. But you need to be sharp and quick with your brain, too. That takes practice, Mac. It takes experience. Most fellows just haven't had enough practice in thinking by the time they are eighteen."

"I can think, sir," Mac said. He wasn't going to give up without a real try. "I finished high school this summer. Class of 1940. I've studied flying, and—"

The sergeant cut in, "I can't sign you up for pilot training, Mac. Rules are rules."

"I didn't know it was a rule, sir."

The sergeant smiled. "That's all right. I don't mind listening to a guy who knows what he wants and has enough spirit to go after it."

Mac laughed. "Well, I guess I'll just wait three more years and then try again."

"There's a better way, Mac."

"What's that?"

"Join the army now," the sergeant answered. "Train to be a soldier. Get most of your marching and digging and stuff like that behind you. Then, when you're twenty-one, you're all ready. If—"

"If? If what, sir?"

"If you pass the tests," the sergeant answered. "It takes a lot to become a flier, Mac. Not everyone can

make the grade. A flier has to have a sharp mind. He has to be in the best of health. If you can pass all the tests of the Air Corps you might make it as a pilot. Some day. It's up to you."

The sergeant sure made it sound like a tough job to become a flier.

"What do you say, Mac?" the sergeant asked. "Want to enlist now? And maybe fly later?"

"If you think that's the best way to do it."

"Good." The sergeant handed Mac some papers to fill out. "No way to be sure. But we need fliers badly. The war in Europe is a long way from being over. If we get into it, we'll need a lot more fliers than we have now."

Mac filled out the army forms and gave them back to the sergeant. "When do I report for duty?" he asked.

"You'll get a notice telling you when and where to report."

"Maybe they will send me to an air base."

The sergeant smiled. "There's not much chance for that, Mac. But you've got the right spirit. Keep it up and I'll bet my sergeant's stripes that one of these days you will be a pilot. Just don't give up."

"I won't," Mac said as he turned to leave. "I sure won't."

THE OLD ONE-TWO
CHAPTER 3

In a few days Mac had his army orders, and was on a bus heading for camp. The bus was crowded with boys all going to the same camp.

At first the boys were quiet as the bus rolled along, taking them farther and farther from home. But after a while they began to talk and laugh. Before the morning was over, all were having a good time together.

That is, all but Al Kroger, a big husky boy in the seat ahead of Mac. No matter what any one said about army life Al always said, "Oh, sure! You know all the answers. Well, some tough sergeant will take that out of you in a hurry."

Long before the bus reached camp that night everyone was tired of listening to Al. But that didn't seem to bother him. He kept right on breaking into their talk, sounding off on everything.

"And what will they make us do?" he asked in a loud

voice. "They'll make us march until we wear our feet off to the knees. Then we'll dig fox holes until we drop. Or pick up paper all over camp. Or—"

Tommy Ross, the boy sitting beside Mac, asked, "What's eating you? Can't you say anything good about the army? If you don't like the army why did you enlist? You're—"

Al whirled around and cut in with, "Who said that?"

Tommy was the smallest boy on the bus, but he answered, "I did. Why?"

"Because I'm going to make your basic training a real happy time, fellow, starting right now. That's why."

He reached out to hit Tommy. As he did, Mac said quietly, "Lay off, fellow. Tommy is my friend."

Just then someone shouted, "The trip is over. There are the gates of our camp."

"Good-by," another boy laughed. "Good-by, free world. Good-by."

A sudden quiet settled over the boys as the bus rolled through the gate and into camp. As far as they could see, army buildings stretched on and on and on.

Mac let out a long, low whistle. "This is some place," he said more to himself than to anyone on the bus. "It's bigger than Dover. Bigger than most cities I have seen."

In many ways the camp was like a city. The wide streets were lined on both sides with buildings. Some of the bigger buildings were the barracks where the soldiers lived. Others were the mess halls where they had their meals. Row upon row of long gray buildings. Street after street.

Following a winding street, the bus at last came to a stop in front of a gray building. An officer hurried out to meet the bus.

"Everyone out!" he called. "This is the end of the line." He pointed to the building. "Inside! Be quick about it."

As Mac started toward the front of the bus, Al took hold of his arm. "I'm not forgetting, fellow," he said. "No one tells Al Kroger to lay off, and gets away with it. You wait. I'll see you later."

Mac nodded but made no answer. He was pretty sure he could take care of himself. Why worry about Al? And besides there was too much to see, too much to do.

In the days that flew by, Mac had little time to think about Al Kroger. He soon found out that there was more to becoming a soldier than just wearing a uniform.

From early morning until dark, Mac and the new boys in camp were kept busy. Every day they marched for miles and miles. Marched until at night in his sleep Mac dreamed of marching.

"Forward march!" the sergeant gave the order. "Left—right—left—right—hup—two—hup—two."

"To the rear—march!"

"Halt—one—two!"

"All right, boys. Let's do it again. Forward march! Left—right—left—right."

And on the days when they weren't marching, there were tests to take. Fox holes to dig. Hours and hours of rifle drill.

Mac had little trouble learning how to use a rifle. In a short time he was a crack shot, the best in his company.

More than once the sergeant said, "You're doing all right, soldier. You have good eyes."

The long weeks, the days, the hours of hard work were paying off. Slowly but surely Mac and the other boys were turning into soldiers.

To be sure, there were those who didn't like army life. And the loudest among them was big, husky Al Kroger.

One day the new soldiers returned to their barracks after a long, hot march. Everyone was bone-tired. They stretched out on their bunks for a short rest before mess call.

Tommy Ross, on the bunk next to Mac, looked over at him and grinned. The march had been harder on Tommy than on the others. His short legs were never meant for marching.

"Mac," he said, "I don't care if I ever get up again. I can't get to the mess hall tonight."

"You'll make it," Mac laughed. "You haven't missed a meal yet."

"I told you guys they would march your legs off," Al Kroger said from his bunk close by.

"We can take it," Mac said.

"Who can take it?" Kroger asked. "Look at Tommy! He can't move."

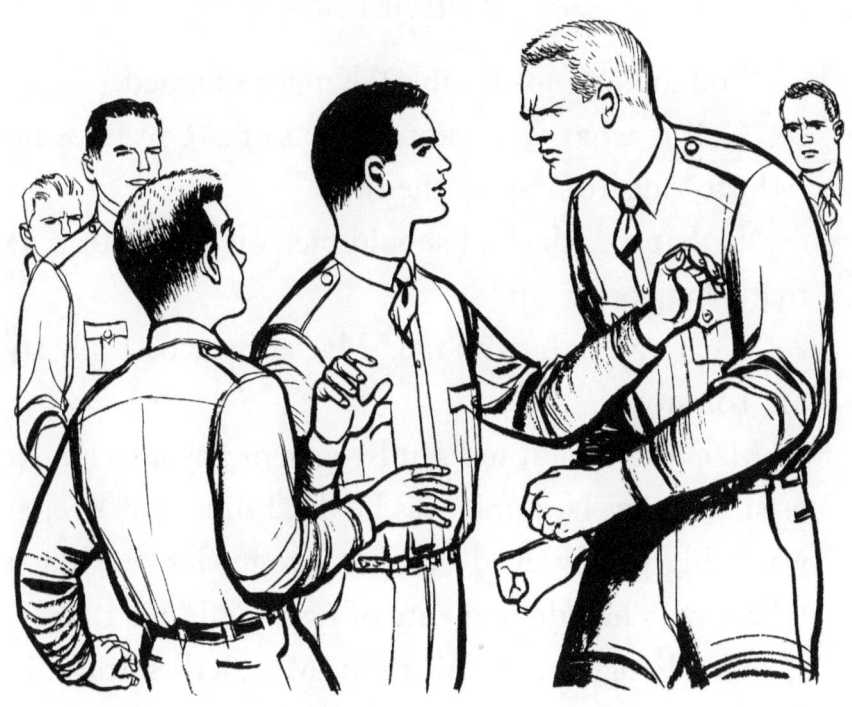

The little fellow shouted, "I'm just as good a soldier as you are."

"Oh, yes? Who says so?"

Tommy jumped to his feet. His face was red as fire. "Cut it out, Kroger. You've been picking on me ever since we got here."

"What are you going to do about it?" Kroger demanded. He got up slowly and came around to the end of the bunk. He stood there towering over little Tommy Ross.

Mac jumped in between them. "Lay off, Kroger," he said. "Tommy's doing as good a job as any of us."

"You looking for trouble?" Kroger snapped.

"Call it what you want," Mac said. "You have no right to ride Tommy all the time."

"Is that so? Maybe I should pick on you instead. Is that what you want?"

"That's all right with me," Mac answered. "Only lay off Tommy."

Mac didn't want to fight Kroger, or anyone else. At least not now. Not only was he dead tired, but Kroger was a big fellow. And besides, Kroger looked like a fellow who had done plenty of fighting in his time.

Now Kroger said, "All right, Mac, let's settle this. How about coming out behind the barracks with me?"

Tommy Ross cut in quickly. "Don't do it, Mac. I'm the one Kroger is after, not you."

"Oh, I don't know," Mac said, making himself smile. "Kroger would be after anybody he thought he could beat."

Kroger's mouth twisted in anger. "You coming, Mac?" he demanded. "Or are you going to stay here where it's safe?"

"I'm right behind you," Mac answered. It was too late to back out now. But then he had not even thought of that.

He turned to Tommy. "You and the others stay here. This is between Kroger and me."

"But, Mac—"

"This is my fight," Mac insisted.

"All right," Tommy gave in. "If that's what you want."

"McConnell doesn't want any of you to see him get whipped," Kroger called back over his shoulder.

Mac followed Kroger from the barracks. They walked around behind the building where no one could see or hear them.

Kroger took off his shirt and tossed it to one side. Mac did the same, all the while noticing Kroger's big muscles.

"I better rush him," Mac told himself. "If I try to box, he'll knock my head off."

So Mac took a deep breath. He held his fists ready, and rushed in.

Pow!

Mac was knocked to the ground. White stars swam in front of his eyes. His jaw hurt. He looked up to see Kroger towering over him.

"What's the matter?" Kroger asked, grinning. "Did you trip over something?"

Mac shook his head without answering. He rolled over and got to his feet.

Pow! Bam!

Down again!

Mac tried to figure out what he was doing wrong. One thing he knew for sure. Instead of hitting, he was getting hit. And you didn't win fights that way.

Then Mac thought of something. It might work. Again it might not. But he had to try it. Or he had to quit right then and there.

"Had enough?" Kroger asked.

"Not quite," Mac said, getting to his feet.

Kroger waited. His fists were held ready.

Mac started back in. He didn't rush. He stepped lightly, and swung with his left hand. Kroger ducked the other way. But Mac barely touched Kroger with his left. He swung hard with his right. Kroger ducked into it.

Bam!

Kroger backed up, holding his nose.

Quickly Mac closed in. Left, right. Left, right. Kroger was caught between Mac's flying fists.

Kroger yelled with anger. Mac hit him again. Left, right. He knocked Kroger down. A look of surprise covered the big fellow's face.

Mac stood over Kroger, his legs spread wide. He waited for Kroger to get up and charge into him again. But the fight had gone out of the big fellow. He got up slowly, forcing a grin.

"Had enough?" It was Mac's turn now to ask the question.

"And how!" Kroger said, breathing hard.

"Let's forget the whole thing," Mac said, holding out a hand. "Shake?"

Kroger paused for a minute. Then as he took Mac's hand he asked, "Say, what did you hit me with when you knocked me down?"

Mac grinned. "The old one-two. Fake with your left. When you get the other fellow ducking away from it, slam him with your right."

Kroger rubbed his face. "Well, I'll say one thing, you sure know how to use it."

"Thanks," Mac said, putting on his shirt. "I learned to box in high school. The old one-two is a good thing to remember. You never know when you might need it."

PILLS, TAGS, AND BAGS OF FLOUR
CHAPTER 4

AL HAD LED the way out behind the barracks. But when the fight was over, Al and Mac walked in together. Everyone in the big room rushed toward them shouting a hundred questions at once.

Mac, with a shake of his head, said, "Forget it, fellows." And that was all they could get out of him.

Al had even less to say. But from then on he made no trouble for anyone.

A few days after the fight Mac was on his way to the mess hall when his sergeant stopped him. The sergeant was a big sun-tanned man with eyes that could drill through an army tank.

"Mac," he said, "I hear you took on Al Kroger the other day."

At first Mac was too surprised to answer. Then he asked, "Did you know about it?"

"There isn't much that goes on in my company that

I don't know about, Mac. But I'll say this, Kroger had it coming."

Then with a friendly slap on the back the sergeant was gone. Mac, watching him walk away, told himself, "He's all right. He's a good Joe. A real good Joe."

The weeks of basic training went on and on. But at last it was over. The weeks of hard work had made quite a change in the young men who had gone through it together. A change for the better. The army had marched and drilled them and turned them into soldiers. Now they were ready to be sent to other camps for more training.

Mac, like the others, stood straight and tall as he waited in line for his orders. He was brown from wind and sun. And there was a new look in his dark eyes, sharp and bright.

Most of the young soldiers were sent to camps for more training with rifles, machine guns, and tanks. Others were sent to radio schools. Al Kroger and some others were to become army cooks. Tommy Ross and Mac were leaving together for special training in an army hospital to help the doctors. They were to become medics. A few who were good mechanics were going to an army flying field to work on airplane engines.

Mac couldn't help saying to Tommy, "They're the

lucky ones. I'd give a lot to be going with them. Being a medic is about as far from being a pilot as anything I can think of right now."

"Pretty hard to fly a box of pills," Tommy said. "But maybe it won't be too bad once you get used to it."

Since he could not be a pilot, Mac had to make the best of it. Almost from the first day he was glad he had been sent to the army hospital. He was needed here. It was a small hospital with never quite enough beds for the sick of a big camp.

Then, too, there were the injured boys brought in from night marches and mock battles. Boys with broken arms and legs. Boys who were sick.

The weeks passed. Weeks of training to become medics. Helping doctors. Taking care of the sick and injured. Giving pills. Writing reports. Putting on bandages and splints. Weeks of hard work.

One night when Mac and Tommy were getting ready to leave the hospital, a doctor stopped them. "Say, what are you fellows doing here? You should have been off duty hours ago."

"I know, Captain," Mac answered. "But the night medics needed a little help and so we stayed on to give them a hand."

The doctor nodded. "You're doing a fine job, boys. But we'll find out how good you really are next week."

"Next week?" Mac asked.

"Yes, that's when the soldiers in camp move out to fight their big mock battle. You two are going along with some other medics to work on the battlefield."

"Yes, sir."

"Next to the real thing this is it, boys. You're in for some rough going."

Mac smiled. "We lived through basic, sir. I guess we can take it all right."

A day or so before the mock battle, Mac with Tommy and ten other medics left camp. Miles out in the hills they set up their field hospital tents. They checked over their medical kits, making sure they had enough pills, bandages, and splints on hand. Mock battle or not, there were sure to be accidents. The medics had to be ready for anything.

Early one morning the captain from the camp hospital arrived. He called the medics together to give them their orders. "The army will be using everything out there, boys. Rifles, tanks, machine guns. Everything but real bullets. But all the same they will run into trouble. You can't fight even a mock battle without some badly injured men. It is up to us to be on the job."

The captain pointed to four men. "You four stay here. Be ready to take care of the soldiers brought in from the field."

He pointed to the others. "The rest of you will be out there with the army. You will work in teams. Get your kits and stretchers and head for the front line."

The captain laughed a little. "And don't ask how to find it. You'll hear where it is once the battle starts. By the way, the soldiers will be wearing arm bands—white for our side, blue for the enemy. But that won't matter to you medics. Take care of the injured, friend and enemy."

"Yes, sir," came from the young medics.

"That's all, men. Get going."

Soon Mac, Tommy, and the six other medics hurried from the field hospital. They had gone about a mile when the sound of gunfire rang out in the woods far to the right.

"It's started," Mac shouted. "The battle is on!"

With Mac in the lead, the medics raced for the woods. The sound of gunfire grew louder.

As they came nearer they could see soldiers running among the trees. Here came a tank, its guns firing away. And here a supply truck rolled down the dusty road, its soldiers firing their rifles at the enemy. Now and then a soldier fell and cried out for a medic.

It was all part of the mock battle plan.

Mac and Tommy worked together as one of the teams. Quickly they answered each cry for help. While one got out his bandages or splints, the other gave the "wounded" soldier a pill.

"Medic," someone called. "Medic."

"Mac, over there," Tommy shouted to make himself heard over the noise of battle. "Another wounded soldier under that tree."

They ran to the soldier lying on the ground. He had a white arm band with a tag tied to it saying, *This soldier has been shot in the left arm.*

Quickly Mac opened his kit to get a bandage. As the soldier took a pill from Tommy he asked, "You going to send me back to a nice soft hospital bed?"

"Sure," Tommy answered. "You're wounded, aren't you?"

The soldier grinned. "Real bad. I guess I'll have to stay in bed while the rest of you are running up and down hills."

He pointed to the stretcher. "How about carrying me back to the field hospital?"

"You can make it on your own," Mac said with a laugh. "You were wounded in the arm, not your feet. Remember?"

"Yes, and you had better get started," Tommy said. "The hospital is about ten miles back in the hills."

"Ten miles! Hey, I'd rather stay here."

While they were talking, a plane flew over the battlefield to drop dummy bombs—bags of flour. One big

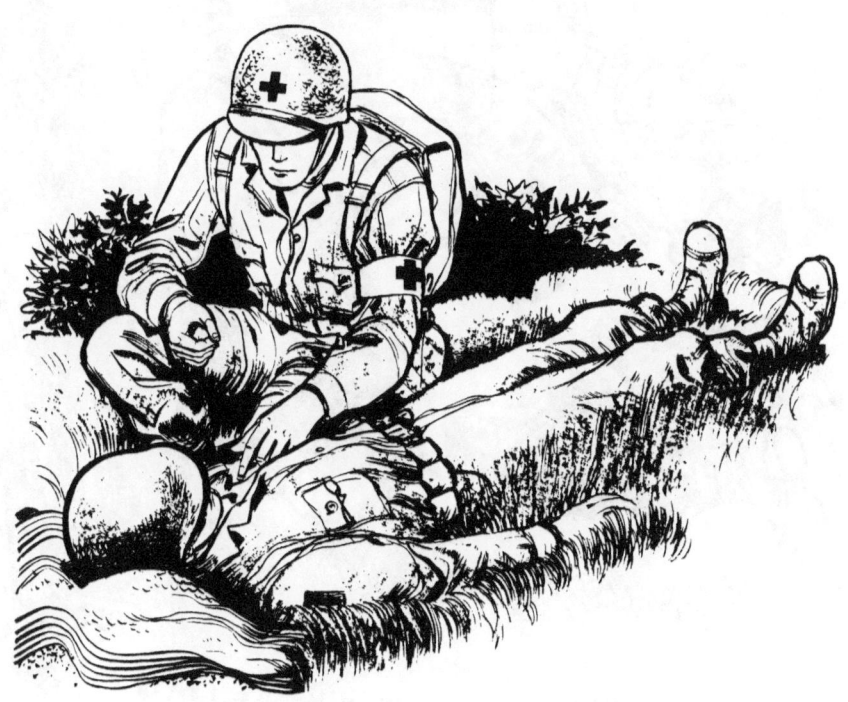

bag came crashing through the trees near by. The flour went flying in all directions.

The soldier let out a cheer. He pointed to some flour on his uniform. "See. You know the rules. Flour on you means you have been killed."

The soldier fell back on the ground. "Now I won't have to make that long walk. Thanks, boys, for trying to save my life. But I'm dead—killed by a bag of flour." He grinned at Mac. Then with a smile on his face he closed his eyes.

Mac and Tommy looked at each other and laughed. "Well, we did what we could," Mac said, picking up his kit.

"Should have saved my pills. And I—"

Tommy's words were drowned out by a loud crash from deep in the woods. For a minute all was quiet. Then cries for help rang out.

The "dead" soldier jumped to his feet. "Say, that sounds too real to be part of the mock battle plans."

"You're right," Mac agreed. "Come on. Let's find out what's going on."

Following a winding road, they ran deeper into the woods. The shouts of "Medic! Medic!" grew louder.

Racing on, they saw that an army truck had run off the road and turned over. Its big wheels were still spinning in the air. On the ground ten or more soldiers lay badly injured.

Mac shot a quick look at Tommy. "This is the real thing, all right."

"It sure is," Tommy said, "and we—"

The soldier with them broke in. "Maybe we should get a doctor."

"A doctor?" Mac asked. "Where? This is our job!"

He opened his kit as he ran to the injured men. "Take it easy, fellows," he said to them. "We're here."

The soldiers, their young faces twisted with pain, looked up at him. Quietly, each waited his turn as Mac and Tommy went from man to man.

Mac worked quickly, but his hands were gentle and sure. It came to him that a medic never knew just what he would be up against on the battlefield.

A medic had to use his head, to think all the time. He had to do the best he could with the few pills, the few bandages and splints he carried in his kit.

Even in real war a medic carried no gun, did no fighting. It went without saying that he was brave. All he had with him on a battlefield was his medicine kit and a prayer.

While Mac and Tommy were caring for the injured men, word of the accident was sent to the field hospital. Soon more medics were on hand to rush the men back to the hospital in the hills.

"We're here to take over," a medic told Mac and Tommy. "Your orders are to stay on the line."

"Sure thing," Mac said. "We're on our way."

As they pushed off, an injured man called to them. "Hey, medics! Thanks. Thanks from all of us."

Mac and Tommy waved their kits in answer. Then they hurried down the dusty road.

"You know," Mac said as they walked along, "you were right about it."

"Right about what?" Tommy asked.

"About being a medic," Mac answered. "You are really doing something when you can help a bunch of good Joes."

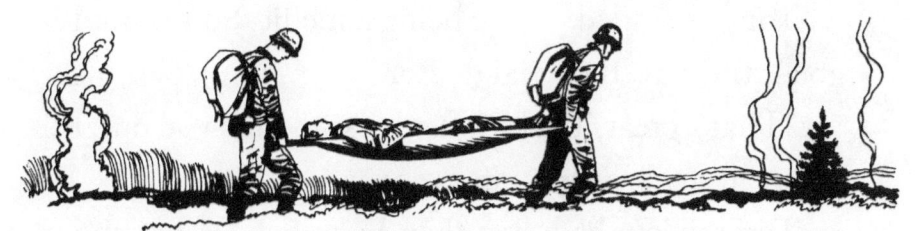

PEARL HARBOR
CHAPTER 5

THE MOCK BATTLE went on for almost two weeks. All the while Mac and Tommy worked together as a team. Time and again they cared for men with "wounded" tags on them. Time and again they saw "dead" soldiers with flour on their uniforms. There were some real accidents, too. Broken arms and legs.

But at last the soldiers with the white arm bands won the battle. After a night of rest the army returned to camp.

Soon after they were back in camp, Mac was ordered to another army hospital. He told Tommy good-by.

"I sure don't like to see you pull out of here," Tommy said. "I'll never forget our being friends."

"That goes for me, too," Mac said. "Good luck, no matter where you go or what you do. Maybe we'll run into each other after we get out of the army. What do you think you'll do then?"

Tommy smiled. "I like being a medic. So I think I'll go all the way. Be a real doctor."

"That's great, Tommy. And just to help you out, I'll bring all my broken bones to you."

Tommy laughed. But then he asked, "What about you, Mac? Still want to be a pilot?"

"That's it, Tommy. Always has been. Always will be."

The army camp where Mac was sent had a fine new hospital. Here he was busy learning new and better ways to care for the sick and injured.

Mac had a way of making friends with everyone. In no time the sick and lonely men waited for the sound of his voice in the long halls. He always had time to write a letter for some lonely boy, far from home. Time to stand by those who were sick. Time to laugh with those who were getting well again.

But he could not make friends with one young soldier. No one could. The soldier, in a room by himself, would talk to no one.

Mac couldn't tell why, but he had a feeling the soldier wasn't sick. The kid was scared. And if someone didn't snap him out of it, he might never get over being scared. He might even turn yellow.

Then one day Mac heard some doctors talking about the soldier. "There is nothing wrong with him," one doctor said. "Nothing shows up in his reports."

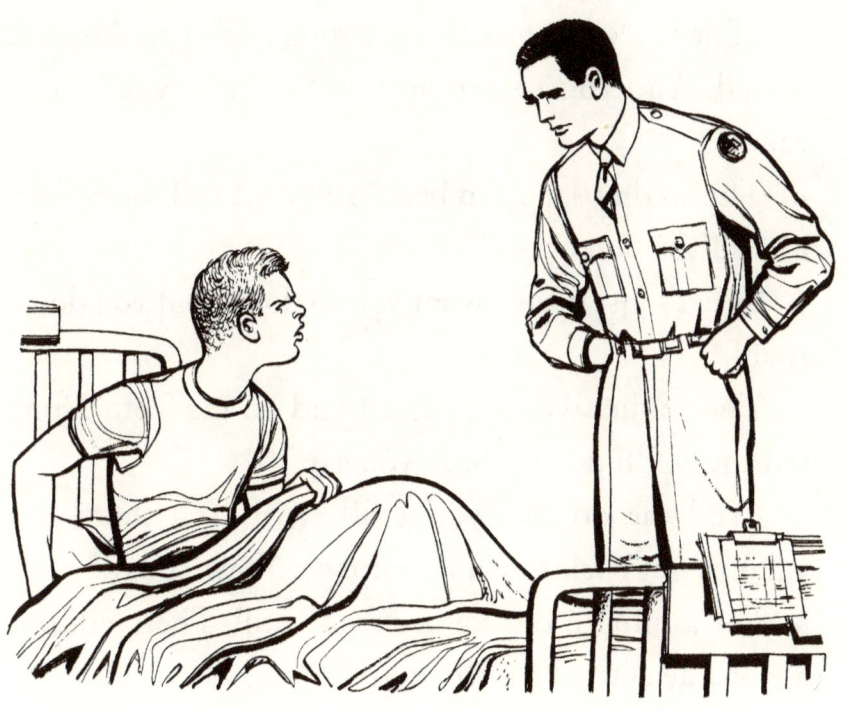

"Think he is faking?" another asked.

"Yes, I do. But to make sure we'll keep him in bed another day or so. Maybe by then he'll snap out of it and we won't have to toss the book at him."

"All right. Let's wait."

Mac knew he had to do something and do it quick. He waited until the doctors went on down the hall. Then he hurried to the soldier's room and closed the door.

"All right, soldier," he said. "On your feet."

The soldier didn't move. He looked up at Mac and asked, "Can't you see I'm sick?"

"There is only one thing wrong with you. You are scared. And you better snap out of it or you'll turn yellow."

The soldier sat up in bed. "You can't call me yellow. I'll tell the doctors—"

"That's just what I want you to do. And if you don't, I will."

The soldier was out of bed and on his feet. "Don't tell them. I'll do anything you say."

"Tell the doctors you're all right. Tell them you want to get back to your company. Now. Today."

For a minute the soldier stood still. Then without a word he started for the door.

Mac watched him hurry down the hall. "Poor kid, I was kind of tough on him. But he'll get over it. He'll be all right."

One Sunday afternoon Mac was off duty. He was in his barracks where some of the fellows were talking. Others were playing games, writing letters home, or sleeping. Still others were listening to the radio. Mac picked up a Sunday paper and stretched out on his bunk to read it.

On a page he saw some pictures of the air war in Europe. Pictures of some English pilots and their planes. There was even one of a German plane with its black crosses.

He read the story of the English crew whose plane had been shot down by the enemy. One by one the men had jumped, bailed out of their flaming plane.

"Boy, that takes nerve," Mac told himself. "Would I have enough nerve to bail out? Maybe I would. Maybe I wouldn't. Guess I'll never really know until—"

All at once Mac was jerked out of his thoughts. Someone had turned up the radio. Everyone in the room had quit what he was doing to listen.

"—this morning," the voice on the radio was saying, "Japan made a sneak attack on Pearl Harbor! Our air fields and most of our planes have been destroyed. Most of our ships have been sunk or badly damaged."

The young soldiers looked at the radio as though they couldn't believe what was coming out of it. Then they looked at one another. No one seemed able to find words to say. It would take them a little while to get over the shock of the terrible news.

Someone coming into the room asked, "What's going on, fellows?"

"Quiet! Listen to the radio."

"Here is word from the Army, the Navy, the Marine Corps," the voice on the radio went on. "All leaves are over. All soldiers, all sailors, all marines return to your posts at once. We repeat—return to your posts at once! Pearl Harbor has been attacked and—"

"Mac, what do you think this means?" one of the fellows asked.

"This is it, fellows," Mac answered. "It means we're in the war."

"We're in, all right," someone else said. "We tried, but we can't stay out of the war any longer. All we have to do now is wait for Congress to declare war on Japan."

All kinds of thoughts whirled through Mac's mind. What would happen now? To America, the country he loved? To him?

Everyone was talking. Mac got up from his bunk to move closer to the radio. As he did, the paper fell to the floor. He picked it up and for the first time he noticed the date on the paper.

Sunday, December 7, 1941—Pearl Harbor! A day for all Americans to remember always!

AIR CADET
CHAPTER 6

WAR! JAPAN'S sneak attack upon Pearl Harbor was a terrible blow to the United States. The bombs that were dropped on the beautiful Pacific harbor did more than kill and destroy. They shocked the nation into action.

The very next day Congress declared war on Japan. A few days later, Japan's allies—Germany and Italy—declared war on the United States.

Now the United States was faced with two wars. A war in Europe. A war in the Pacific. Ready or not, this was a fight to the finish.

Americans everywhere answered their country's call to arms. But as the months passed, Japan took over more islands in the Pacific. One heart-breaking defeat followed another.

In Europe things were no better. Germany's giant

war machine had rolled over Western Europe and was out to rule the world.

In the months since Pearl Harbor, Mac worked hard as a medic. Sure, he was doing his part. Yet the feeling stayed with him that he could help more as a pilot in the Army Air Corps.

But war or no war, a fellow had to be twenty-one before he could sign up for pilot training. And so Mac waited out the time. At last in January of 1943 he was twenty-one. He lost no time in filling out the needed forms and sent them off to the Air Corps.

More months passed. Spring came and went. Summer was over. And still no word.

Then one fall day Mac was on his way to the hospital with some of the other medics. He heard someone call to him, "Hey, Mac, the CO wants to see you."

The CO! The Commanding Officer of the camp!

"What have you been up to, Mac?" a medic asked. "Have you—"

"Maybe the CO has news for you," broke in another. "News from the Air Corps."

A quick smile flashed across Mac's face and then it was gone. "No such luck," he said. "Not after all these months. I guess I'm just in for another move."

Mac was partly right. He was being sent to another camp.

"We're sorry to lose a good medic," the CO told him. "But you're to report for training at Washington State College."

Mac's heart missed a beat or two. "Washington State?" he asked. "At Pullman? The Air Corps has a school there, sir."

The CO nodded. "That's right. And that's where you're going. You'll be an air cadet."

Mac let out a shout, then caught himself. "Sorry, sir."

"It's all right," the CO said with a smile. "You have waited a long time for these orders."

"Yes, sir. A long time."

"Good luck, soldier."

"Thank you, sir."

A few days later Air Cadet Joseph McConnell, Jr. reported for training at Washington State College. Washington State was not a flying school. It was a ground school. Like other ground schools of the Air Corps, its job was to get the cadets ready to fly.

"Hi, there," a young cadet said, stepping up to Mac.

"Hi."

"I'm Chip Logan." The cadet held out a big hand. "Chip Logan, Air Cadet."

As they shook hands Mac said, "I'm Joe McConnell, Air Cadet."

They both laughed. This air cadet business was great.

"Come along, Mac. Meet the rest of the fellows. We'll have a good time tonight. But in the morning school starts. Then we're in for it."

"That's all right with me," Mac said. "The sooner we get started, the sooner we'll be out of ground school. I can't wait to climb into a fighter plane and go whizzing through the wild blue sky."

Chip slapped Mac on the back. "So you're all set to be a pilot."

"Sure, aren't you?"

"Boy, I hope so. But not all of us will make it. Some will wash out. Others will wind up as navigators or bombardiers or—"

"Maybe that's all right for some fellows," Mac said. "But I'm going to be a pilot. A fighter pilot."

Mac and the other young cadets had a good time together that first night, getting to know one another. But they were up early the next morning, ready for their first class.

They were marched out to one of the college buildings where a small training plane was parked. An Air Corps captain was waiting beside the plane. He looked them over, one by one, and shook his head.

"We're here to teach you fellows something about

flying," he began. "Looking at you, I can see it's going to be a tough job."

Mac smiled.

"Wipe that smile off your face," the officer snapped. "You stand a pretty good chance of being the first one to wash out."

Mac held his breath. All he had done was to smile a little.

"The Air Corps has no time for men who can't take it," the captain went on. "You'll learn to fly or you'll be washed out. It's as simple as that. Any questions?"

"No, sir. No, sir," came from the listening cadets.

"What? No questions?" the officer asked in mock surprise. He shook his head again. "Every class gets better and better. Pretty soon there will be no need for ground school."

Mac kept his eyes straight ahead. "This is all part of the game," he told himself. "Trying to make us jumpy. Go ahead, Captain, you can't make me step out of line again."

The captain moved in closer to the plane. He nodded to the cadets, then pointed to the ground. "That which you are standing on is the ground," he told them without cracking a smile. "All flying starts and ends there."

He pointed up over his head. "That above you is the sky. It reaches from the ground to—to the stars. You will be doing your flying between these two—ground and stars. Is that clear?"

It was clear that the captain was doing his best to kid the cadets. But Mac didn't even smile. No, sir, he had learned one lesson.

"All right." The officer walked around to the front of the plane. "Now we'll go on. This is an airplane. In order to fly, it needs a pilot. But even more important, in order for a pilot to fly he needs an airplane. That's why it's a good idea for you and the airplane to know each other. Know everything about each other."

"Now we're getting down to business," Chip said quietly to Mac.

Mac nodded, but made no other answer.

The captain put his hand on the propeller.

"This is a propeller, men. Until we get some other kind of plane—like the jets you may have heard about—you will need a prop to pull you through the sky. Now this—"

It went on that way. Propeller. Wings. Cockpit. Control stick. Rudder. So much to learn.

In the days that followed, the cadets went from one class to another. All day and every day was the same. But they didn't mind the hard work and the long hours of study.

In class the cadets learned the call letters and codes used by the Air Corps. They learned to make maps and to read them. Maps of the country, the weather. They spent hours working with radios. Hours with guns. Hours studying airplane instruments and engines.

Days, weeks of hard work. Days, weeks of study. Tests and more tests. Books and more books. Maps and charts. Instruments and engines.

Day after day the lessons went on and on. Along with their flying lessons, the cadets learned what it meant to be good officers.

They not only studied hard and worked hard—they played hard.

"You have to keep your body in top shape to stay in the Air Corps," their captain told them. "A good strong body helps keep your mind sharp. There is no place in a plane for anyone with a weak body or a slow mind. Let it happen to you and I'll wash you out fast. We want tigers in our planes!"

The weeks passed. At last the day came when

ground school was over. The cadets who hadn't washed out were ready to go on.

When the orders were posted Mac called, "Hurry up, Chip. Let's see where we go for our pilot training."

They rushed down the hall to find out about their orders.

"I made it," Chip called. "I'm being sent on for pilot training!"

"That's great. Great!" Mac ran his finger down the list.

He came to his own name. The smile on his face was gone.

"McConnell, Jr., Joseph," he read. "Hondo Air Base …Navigation School."

"What's the matter?" Chip asked, looking at him closely.

"I didn't make it," Mac said in a low voice. "I didn't make it. They're sending me to Hondo to become a navigator."

"Nothing wrong with being a navigator," Chip said. "Without a navigator a bombing plane would never reach its target, or find its way back home."

"Yes, I know. But it's not being a pilot. I want to be a pilot. A pilot. A pilot!"

"You'll be flying, Mac."

"Oh, sure. But not in a fast little fighter plane. They'll put me in a big bomber like a Liberator. They'll give me some charts and maps and I'll sit at a little table, and—and—"

Mac could say no more. He tried to smile. It just wouldn't come.

All the work, the weeks of study had gone for nothing. Nothing. They still wouldn't let him be a pilot.

It was almost more than he could take.

FLYING SCHOOL
CHAPTER 7

HONDO AIR BASE was in Texas. Almost from the first Mac liked Hondo. That is, he liked it after he got over being sorry he didn't make the grade for pilot training.

"If I can't be a pilot," he told himself, "I'll be the best navigator they ever had. At least, I'll try."

Mac and the other cadets at Hondo studied hard to become navigators. Once again it was books and more books. Maps. Charts. Instruments.

In class Mac learned how to read the stars to guide him. He learned about winds and how they could blow a plane miles off its course. He learned to plan a flight, using the winds to help him.

The lessons were very hard. A few more cadets washed out. A couple of times when Mac made mistakes he was afraid he might be washed out, too.

But a training officer told him, "Everyone makes

mistakes, McConnell. We won't wash you out for one or two. Maybe for even more. Just don't make the same mistake twice!"

Mac didn't. Before long he began to take training flights in a Liberator bomber. The Liberator, with its crew of ten or eleven men, was one of the Air Corps' biggest and best bombers. It had four big engines and the biggest wing spread Mac had ever seen. The Liberator could carry a heavy load of bombs and fly at a speed of around two hundred miles an hour.

One day Mac was signed to fly a practice mission with his crew on the Liberator. "This will be a mock battle," the crew was told. "You may be attacked by some of our fighter planes from another air base. Today they are enemy planes. Watch out for those 'bandits.' Don't let them shoot you down. Of course, your guns and theirs will not be shooting bullets but will be shooting pictures of one another. But don't think it's just a game. In another month or so you may be in the real thing."

The crew, from pilot to tail gunner, nodded. "Yes, sir."

"That's all, men. Talk over the plans for your mission. Remember, it's teamwork that counts."

Mac and the rest of the crew got out their charts and maps. They checked over the course they were to fly. They made sure their oxygen masks were in working order. High up where they would be flying there wouldn't be enough oxygen in the thin air to keep a man alive.

They practiced calling out the "clock" code used by airmen to find or point out anything in the sky. No matter what direction the plane was flying—north, south, east, or west—its nose always pointed toward "twelve o'clock." "Six o'clock" was straight behind the tail of the plane. If someone called, "Bandits at nine o'clock," you looked straight out to your left. For "Three o'clock low" you looked straight to your right and down. It went that way, all around the clock. It was a simple, easy way to spot anything without having to search all over the sky for it.

Two flights of four big bombers each were made ready to fly the practice mission. One flight was given the code name Blue Flight, the other was Red Flight.

One by one the heavy bombers took off into the sky spotted with soft white clouds. Mac flew in the lead plane of Blue Flight. He sat at his little chart table up near the nose of the plane. He put on his oxygen mask and made sure the radio wire leading to his head phones was working.

Then he turned to his maps to check the course he had laid out. He sure didn't want to make any mistakes on his first mission. He heard the pilot call over the

intercom system used by the crew to talk to one another. "Time for a mike check, fellows. Roger in, if you read me."

The ten members of the crew checked in one at a time, starting at the nose of the plane and working back to the tail gunner.

"Bombardier. Read you loud and clear, pilot."

"Navigator, roger," Mac said.

"Co-pilot, roger."

"Flight engineer, roger."

"Radio operator, roger."

The four gunners checked in, each giving his position.

"Mike check finished," the pilot said. "OK, Mac, take us to the target, boy. You other fellows keep a sharp lookout for bandits. Don't let them get the drop on us."

Mac looked out the small window at his side. The clouds had become thicker, spreading out below the plane like a great white rug. For an hour or so the planes flew high above the clouds. All the while Mac was checking over his maps, charts, and figures. Every once in a while he talked over the intercom to the pilot, asking him to make a change in direction.

"Fifty miles from target," he told the pilot at last. "Right on course."

"Nice going, Mac. All right, bombardier, get your bombsight ready. As soon as Mac gets us to our final check point, you tell us how you want to fly the bomb run."

"Roger," came the bombardier's quick answer. Once the plane was on the bomb run he was in command. The pilot would speed up, slow down, or change course only on orders from the bombardier.

"Thirty miles from target," Mac said a while later. He checked his map to find the small town over which they were passing. "Be at the final check point in about five minutes."

"I'm watching, Mac," the bombardier said over the intercom. "As soon as—"

"Bandits! Ten o'clock high!" An excited voice cut in on the intercom.

"Bandits! Ten o'clock high!" the pilot repeated. "Get your guns ready, fellows."

Mac looked out the window to his left. There were the bandits—enemy planes—diving down upon the bombers.

"Ten o'clock high!"

The sky seemed full of diving planes and roaring engines. Gunners on each crew tried to "shoot" down the bandits with their gun cameras.

The mock air battle went on for a few miles high

up in the sky. The fighter planes zoomed and dived among the bombers. But soon the tiny fighters ran low on gas and turned back toward their home air base.

"Good going," the pilot's voice came over the intercom. "Now back to work."

Mac, busy at his table, went over his map once more. "Final check point," he called to the bombardier.

"Roger," the bombardier answered as he took over the bomb run. Carefully he checked his sights and called out his directions to the pilot.

"Bomb bay doors open!" the bombardier commanded.

The heavy doors rolled open.

Time seemed to stand still. Then at last the target was almost beneath them.

"Bombs away!" the bombardier called out.

Mac watched the stick of dummy bombs tumble from the open bomb bay and fall from sight. No sooner were the bombs away than the pilot once again took over command of the big bomber.

"Lead us home, Mac," he called.

That night the men got together to study the pictures of the mock battle. Mac's crew was told, "You fellows were shot down almost ten miles before reaching your target."

The men looked at the pictures taken by the gun cameras of the fighter planes. There they were—right in the middle of the sights.

"Boy, oh, boy!" Mac said. "Look at us! If that fighter had been shooting real bullets we would have had to bail out—those of us who were still alive."

"You fellows need a lot more training," an officer said. "Maybe the mission should have been planned so you would fly lower. Flying low makes it tough for enemy fighters to dive down on you without crashing into the ground."

"Sure," the pilot said. "But when you fly low you run into trouble with enemy gunners on the ground."

"As for me," the co-pilot said, "I'd rather be shot at when I'm up high. At least, if you get hit you have a chance to bail out."

"Not me," another said. "In a real war the flak from anti-aircraft guns gets so thick that you can almost get out and walk on it. When flak is that thick your chances of getting through safely are pretty thin."

Everyone began talking, trying to figure out how they might have made the mission without being shot down. Everyone tried to figure out what they had done wrong. Then they would know what to do on the next mission. And how to do it better.

"They sure expect us to learn a lot in a few months' time," someone said. "Why, it takes years to learn all that stuff!"

"We don't have years," Mac said. "With a war going on in Europe and in the Pacific, we don't have time. Germany and Japan are making it tough for us and our allies. We are needed badly. They have to get us ready. Quick."

And so the cadets worked over their books and maps. Soon the training flights got longer.

Mac flew more and more in the Liberator. "I'm sure to end up as a navigator on a Liberator," he told himself. And he had learned to like the idea. The Liberator was a good plane.

Another thing that Mac liked was the teamwork of the crew members. Each man of the crew worked together with the others or the mission failed.

Practice, practice, and more practice. Slowly Mac became a whiz at navigation. Day or night he was able to guide a plane over hundreds of miles. He never missed the target they were to reach. Different pilots asked for him to be put on their crews.

"McConnell," his training officer told him, "keep up the good work. Before long you'll be getting your navigator wings."

This was good news to Mac.

Finally the day came when Mac was graduated. He and the others in his class were made lieutenants. They were given their navigator wings and ordered to report to another air base for the last of their training.

"Think we'll ever make it, Mac?" a new young lieutenant asked. "I mean, think we'll get out in time to fight in this man's war?"

"Sure," Mac answered. "We'll be on our way in no time. The only thing that could go wrong now would be for them to keep us here as training officers."

THE LONG HOP
CHAPTER 8

For the last of their training, Mac and the young lieutenants reported to a crew training center. Here, hundreds of other airmen also were winding up their long months of training.

"By now you men know your jobs," the instructor told them. "You know because you've had it drilled into you all along the line. But you still have one more thing to learn and that's why you're here. You're going to learn to work with the crew you'll be flying with from now on."

Mac couldn't help but grin. The Air Corps didn't spend weeks letting a guy work with a crew and then make him stay at home as a training officer. No, sir, this was it! They were training to fly off to war.

"A crew is nothing more than a team of men working together," the instructor went on. "The better the teamwork, the better the crew. But teamwork takes practice, and that's what you're going to do here. You're going to practice teamwork, teamwork, and more teamwork."

The names of the men making up each crew were read off. One by one, they lined up to get their orders. Mac was signed on a Liberator crew along with nine other men. The pilot of Mac's plane was a young lieutenant named Lee Evans. There was something about the quick, sure way Evans took over that Mac liked. He had a feeling that the tall, friendly pilot was a good man to have commanding the bomber in case of trouble.

"Let's make ours a good crew," Evans said to his men. "You know, the instructor is right. It's teamwork that counts. So let's give this last stretch of training everything we have."

"Yes, sir," came from the crew.

Andy Mingin, one of the waist gunners, said, "We're with you, Lieutenant. We're with you all the way."

The crew was made up of four officers and six enlisted men. At first they spent most of their time getting to know one another. They studied together and worked together.

Time and again they flew out on practice missions. They flew by day, in storms or in clear weather. They

flew by night when the stars were bright. And on other nights when the clouds hid most everything from sight. They fought their mock air battles high in the sky, and dropped dummy bombs on far-off targets.

Day by day they trained together, learning to work as a team. Over and over the lessons of teamwork were drilled into them. But they were still a green crew, a crew that tried too hard. They had yet to learn that teamwork was like breathing. You did it without thinking.

Then one day when they were flying home from a practice mission, Andy was taken sick.

Quickly Mac spoke into the intercom. "Navigator to pilot."

"Pilot," came the answer.

"I had better go back and look at Andy."

"Stay at your desk," Lee ordered. "Can't take the chance of getting off our course. We'll get Andy back to the base as soon as we can."

"Roger."

"Pilot to radio man. Do you read me?"

"I hear you loud and clear, sir," the radio operator answered over the intercom.

"Call the base," Lee Evans said. "Tell them to have a medic meet us when we land."

Mac was kept busy with his charts and figures. About an hour later the big bomber was over the airfield. Within minutes after landing, Andy was being rushed to the base hospital.

Mac and the other members of the crew checked in, and that night they looked over the pictures of their flight. It had been a good mission. The bombardier had hit the target right on the button. But there was no kidding around. One of their crew was sick. Good old Andy. Until he was back at his gun again—well, flying wouldn't be the same without him.

A week passed. A week of study and ground work. Then Andy was back with the crew. Once more all was well. Grinning like so many school boys, the men took off on another practice run.

"Pilot to crew," Lee called out on the intercom. "Let's have our mike check."

One by one the men gave their positions. Bombardier. Navigator. Co-pilot. Flight engineer. Radio operator. The gunners.

The same old roll call, checking in to be sure that everything was in order. But today there was something different in their quick answers. A snap in each man's voice. Maybe it was just because they were flying together again.

Soon the long months of training were over. Early in the year of 1945 the crew, along with most of the others at the base, was ordered to England.

"I hear some of the crews are flying over in their own planes," Mac said to Lee. "Are we that lucky?"

The pilot shook his head. "No, I wish we were. I'm used to the old girl. But we're making the long hop in a transport plane with some other fellows from the field. We'll pick up our Liberator over there."

Mac gave Lee a slap on the back. "Well, it's the crew that counts. As long as we stay together, we can fly any plane they give us."

"Right you are!"

The day the men left for England was cold and cloudy. The men were quiet as the flying miles took them farther and farther from home and loved ones.

Hour after hour, the plane flew on its course with only the clouds above, the blue ocean below.

All at once one of the transport's four engines started to pop and smoke. The plane began to lose altitude.

Word was sent back by the pilot. "Take it easy, men. But be ready in case we have to ditch."

"Ditch?" someone yelled. "You mean land out here in the middle of the ocean?"

"Not if you can find us a nice dry landing field," a crew member said, smiling. "Besides, don't worry. We're still in the air, aren't we?"

Before long the engineers had the engine running smoothly again.

The sun set, and the sky grew dark. The men went to sleep in their seats. The plane flew on and on.

Once during the night they landed on an island. Time out for fuel. Time out for the men to eat and then fly on. Once again the engines hummed smoothly as they flew on through the black sky.

It was morning when Mac opened his eyes again. The ocean lay shining in the sunlight. At times it was

dark with the shadows of high clouds racing along with the plane.

Mac turned to Lee. "Beautiful, isn't it? Makes it hard to believe there's a war going on."

Sometime in the afternoon land was sighted. England! The long hop was almost over.

The plane flew lower, heading for an airfield. Coming in over the land, the young men had their first look at a bombed city. Hardly a building or house was still standing. There were great holes in the streets. They could see where fires had burned and raged.

Lee pointed down to the bombed city. "It's not hard to believe there's a war going on now."

Mac nodded. "We're in for a bigger job than I ever dreamed about, Lee. This must never happen to our country."

CREW OF THE SCREAMING EAGLE
CHAPTER 9

SOON AFTER they landed, Mac and the rest of the crew went out to see their new plane. Talking and laughing, they headed across the field for their Liberator, lined up with some others near the runway. One look at the big bomber and their grins were gone.

No one needed to tell the crew the Liberator had taken part in some tough missions. Her great brown painted wings had been patched in many places to cover up bullet holes. Other holes had been patched up, too. Holes made by flak, pieces of metal from the anti-aircraft guns.

For a while no one spoke. At last Lee turned to his crew. "I can't say she's much for looks, fellows. But they tell me she flies like a bird."

"I'm sure she does, sir," one of the gunners added. "Best of all, she's ours."

The others took up the cry. She was theirs and that settled it.

Sure, the Liberator was like any other when you just looked at her. She had the same number of parts, the same number of everything. Still, she wasn't really like any other plane in the sky. No, sir! Your plane was always the best one. There was no way to explain this. It was just so. Like your crew, it was the best. Like your folks always being the best in the world. Like your best girl.

Mac checked the airplane carefully. "She's not much for looks," he said. "That's for sure. Still, I'll bet she can go screaming through the sky like an eagle. And I'll bet she gets us where we want to go and brings us back home again."

Lee Evans smiled. He reached out and gave the plane a pat. "That's right, Mac," he said. "And I like that screaming eagle part. What do you say we name her the *Screaming Eagle*? OK, crew?"

"Sure," the men agreed, laughing. "That's our plane. The *Screaming Eagle!*"

During the next few days the crew of the *Screaming Eagle* made their practice runs over England. As on real missions, little fighter planes flew with them, keeping a sharp watch for trouble.

The time came at last when they were ordered out on the first bombing mission against the enemy. In the briefing room everyone was tense and excited. The men were told what their mission was to be. They were given the latest weather reports, radio code calls, and other matters important in carrying out the mission.

They were told to wear their Mae West life jackets. If they had to parachute from a crippled plane into the cold water of the English Channel, the Mae Wests would hold them up until help arrived.

When the briefing was over, the crew of the *Screaming Eagle* headed for their plane. Each man climbed inside and took his place.

Mac sat down at his small table behind the bombardier. He spread out his charts and maps, then looked around. Everything was much the same as it had been during their practice training bomb runs.

But one thing was different. Then the bomb bay in the middle of the plane had been loaded with dummy bombs. Today they were real.

Lee taxied the Liberator to the end of the runway. He waited his turn in line while the planes ahead of him took off.

At last his orders came from the control tower and he pushed the throttle full forward. Slowly the Liberator picked up speed as it rolled down the runway. But it was so heavy with bombs that it didn't seem able to leave the ground.

"Will we make it?" Mac asked himself. Yet, he knew that if anyone could get that plane off the ground, Lee Evans could do it.

The four giant engines roared. But the spinning wheels were still on the runway.

"Up!" Mac cried to himself, as though his words might help Lee. "Up!"

The plane was nearly to the end of the runway. Almost into the trees.

At the last moment, Lee pulled back on the control wheel with all his might. The plane wobbled for a moment, then lifted into the air, barely missing the tree tops.

Before long the *Screaming Eagle* joined the other planes and headed across the English Channel, toward Germany. Small, fast fighter planes flew above them, making white vapor trails in the sky. But the fighter escorts, with their small gas tanks, had a short range. Soon they had to turn back toward their home fields. Now the bombers were alone.

"Mac, where are we?" Lee Evans called.

"About twenty minutes from Germany," Mac answered into the intercom.

"OK. Everybody keep a sharp eye out for enemy fighters. They'll be looking for us."

Suddenly one of the bomber's engines began to knock and smoke. The flight engineer quickly shut it off, and studied the engine instruments.

"What's up?" Lee Evans asked over his shoulder.

"Looks pretty bad, sir," the flight engineer answered. "Afraid the engine is cracked."

"We're losing altitude fast," the co-pilot said. "Three engines aren't enough to carry our heavy load of bombs."

"We'll have to head back for our base," Lee Evans agreed, already starting to turn the plane. "But we'll have to drop our bombs before we land. We can make it home on three engines without our bomb load."

The radio operator told the other planes about the *Screaming Eagle's* trouble, and why it was dropping out of the mission. "Good luck," the word came back.

When the *Screaming Eagle* was over the English Channel again, Lee ordered the bomb bay doors opened.

"Drop your bombs," he called to the bombardier.

Mac, looking down, saw the bombs hit and explode in the water.

They were still over the Channel when something streaked past them. Mac never had seen anything fly as fast.

"Hey," he yelled over the intercom, "what was that?"

"Don't know," Lee Evans shouted. "But it was sure going like blue blazes!"

"Here it comes again! Wow! What kind of plane do you call that?"

"I thought I saw a black cross painted on it."

"Then it's a German plane," Mac shouted. "Watch out, fellows."

The plane whizzed past again. Bullets streaked from its nose, just missing the Liberator.

"He's going too fast to get a good shot at us," the bombardier called into the intercom.

By now the Liberator's guns were chattering as the waist and tail gunners tried to hit the enemy plane. Their bullets fell far short.

"Hey, that thing doesn't have a propeller," a gunner shouted.

No propeller! A picture jumped into Mac's mind.

"It's a jet!" he cried. "One of those new German jets we've heard about!"

The plane flashed past once again. The speedy jet kept on going and soon it was out of sight.

"He must be getting low on fuel," Evans said. "Probably has to hurry back to his airfield."

"Boy," Mac said, "he must have been going five hundred miles an hour! I hope the Germans don't have many of those things. We haven't a plane fast enough to stop a jet."

Before long they were back over their field, wobbling along on three engines. They made a rough landing, but no one said anything about it. They were all too glad to be back safe.

"You fellows are lucky," the field mechanics said later, after looking over the *Screaming Eagle's* cracked engine. "It's a wonder the whole engine didn't fly to pieces. You'll have to wait a few days before she is ready to fly again."

"A few days?" Mac asked.

"Don't push your luck, Lieutenant," a mechanic said. "You'll have time to fly plenty of missions before this war is over."

BANDITS AROUND THE CLOCK
CHAPTER 10

WHILE THE *Screaming Eagle* was grounded, Mac spent most of the time in the briefing room. He heard the crews going out on missions get their orders and wished he were going along.

More than once Mac watched the young airmen head for their waiting planes. He heard them talk and laugh with one another, even though there was plenty to worry about on every flight. But they were over here to do a job. It was as simple as that. Only, of course, it really wasn't simple at all. He knew, and so did they, that some of them might not come back. Only a few times did all the planes going out on a mission get back to their home base. Yet, no one talked about it. Even though the feeling was there all the time.

Late one morning when Mac was on his way to the briefing room, Lee Evans called to him. "Hi, Mac, I've been looking for you. The *Screaming Eagle* is ready and we're on the books to fly today."

Mac grinned. "Good."

"We're taking off in an hour."

"I'm ready now," Mac said.

"You're always ready," Lee laughed. "Let's go."

At the briefing they were told that the mission would be to bomb a German city where airplane parts were made.

"We must knock out their factories," the squadron CO said. "Cut off their supply of parts and they won't be able to keep their fighters in the sky."

An hour later, right on time, the *Screaming Eagle* was in the air. With Lee at the controls, the big brown plane headed across the channel to Germany. They ran into a few German fighters, but got through them and bombed their target. They were back at their home base by night.

Every few days after that the *Screaming Eagle* was sent out with other Liberators on bombing missions. Time and again they ran into trouble with the German fighter planes. The fast little fighters, their machine guns blazing, dived down upon the big slow bombers. The Liberator gunners shot down some of the enemy planes. But all too often a Liberator went down in flames. All too often the words "Failed to return" were posted in the briefing room.

On one mission when the *Screaming Eagle* was over Germany, the air suddenly was full of popping sounds. POP-POP-POP-POP.

"Hold on, boys," Lee called over the intercom. "Here comes the flak."

On the ground far below, German gunners were firing anti-aircraft shells up at them. Every so often a shell exploded near the plane. Each time the bomber was tossed about as though it had been slapped by a giant hand.

Mac looked out the small window beside him. He could see black puffs of smoke all over the sky. Some were close to the other bombers in the group. Each exploding puff threw metal flak into the air. When pieces of flak hit the plane, it sounded like hail on a tin roof.

"Man alive," the co-pilot shouted, "did you ever see so much flak? Now I believe the guy who said you could almost get out and walk on it."

Just then Mac saw a Liberator in the group tip up on its side and slowly nose down in a dive. "Someone's hit!" he cried out over the intercom.

Flames poured from the crippled bomber, making a smoky, dark streak in the sky. The bomber's wing snapped like the wing of a wounded bird.

Mac saw the crew start to bail out one by one. He counted six bodies tumbling through the air. Then he saw six parachutes open before the plane was out of sight.

He prayed that the others got out in time.

"Bandits!" the radio operator's voice shouted into the intercom. "Bandits at nine o'clock high!"

Mac turned to the window on his left and looked up. The enemy fighter planes were dots in the sky. They came diving down on the group of bombers.

"Mac, keep us on course," Lee Evans called quickly. "Gunners, take care of those babies!"

It was all Mac could do to keep his eyes and mind on his instruments. But that was his job. He felt helpless sitting at his table, bracing himself against the bullets he hoped would never come.

All around him machine guns chattered. RAT-TAT-TAT-TAT-TAT-TAT-TAT-TAT—

"Got him!" a voice yelled. "I got one of them!"

"There he goes! He's on fire!"

"Good shooting," Lee called to the gunner.

Mac wiped the sweat from his face. Lee and his co-pilot were holding the *Screaming Eagle* on a straight course. Near the nose of the Liberator the bombardier was working over his bombsight, getting ready for the bomb run.

"Here comes another bandit!" Andy shouted from his gunner position. "Two of them! Low. Six o'clock low! Watch them, tail gunner!"

"I see them. Here they come!"

RAT-TAT-TAT-TAT-TAT-TAT-TAT-TAT—

"Missed both of them!" The tail gunner let out an angry shout.

Suddenly Andy's voice came over the intercom. "I'm hit! He got me!"

Bullets came crashing through the Liberator. One shot left a big hole above Mac's head.

But he went on with his work, even though the battle was raging all around him. "Ten minutes from target!" he called.

"Good going, Mac," the bombardier said. "Bombardier to crew. Get those bomb bay doors open and ready."

"Roger."

The big bomb bay doors rolled open.

Mac got up from his desk and climbed to the flight deck where Lee Evans and his co-pilot were busy at the controls.

"Lee, if you stick to this course you'll make the target all right."

"Good," the pilot said. "But what are you going to do, Mac?"

"I'm going to check Andy. I'll be back by the time we've finished the bomb run."

"Think you can make it?" Lee Evans asked. "With

the bomb bay doors open, it will be hard to get back to him."

"I have to make it," Mac answered quickly.

"Andy's in pretty bad shape, I think," the other waist gunner cut in on the intercom.

"Do you know what to do, Mac?"

"I should. I was a medic."

"OK, go to it. But be sure to keep your oxygen with you. We're at twenty thousand feet, you know."

Carrying the round metal "bottle" filled with oxygen, Mac started toward the rear of the plane. Reaching the metal wall that separated the bomb bay from the flight deck, he paused. He looked through the narrow opening. A shiver went through him. Below the open bomb bay doors there was only empty space—and the ground far below.

"Lieutenant, where are you going?" the flight engineer yelled as Mac put down the oxygen bottle and began to take off his parachute.

Mac shouted above the blast of the wind smashing into the bomb bay. "Back to Andy. Can't make it with my parachute on. Too big, and—"

"Let me go."

"Your job is to keep those engines running."

"But, sir—"

"That's an order," Mac called over his shoulder. He

put on his mask again and picked up the oxygen bottle. Slowly he squeezed through the small doorway into the bomb bay.

Mac took one look at the long narrow metal walk he had to cross in order to reach Andy. One thing for sure, there was plenty of empty space between the metal catwalk and the ground below. Twenty thousand feet of it!

He took a deep breath and stepped into the bomb bay. The wind smashed against him. But he went on, step by step, holding on to anything he could reach. He glanced down just once. If he lost his footing—he tried not to think about that!

Slowly, small step by small step, he moved along the narrow catwalk, bracing himself against the steady blast of the wind.

Once his foot slipped. Quickly he reached for one of the racks that held the bombs in place. For a moment he was over empty space before he could get his feet back on the catwalk. He paused and breathed deeply once more. He went on until he came to the doorway that led into the gunners' space and squeezed through the small opening.

Andy lay in a huddle on the cold metal floor. The other gunner was busy at his guns. He had done all he could for Andy. And he had seen to it that the wounded man's oxygen mask was in place.

Andy looked up at Mac. "I—I'm all right, sir." It was all he could do to talk over the intercom. "Just a scratch."

"It's more than a scratch," Mac said. "Now you lie still."

"But my gun, sir. I must get back to it."

"I know. But I'll take over for you."

As soon as Andy's shoulder was bandaged, Mac jumped to the machine guns sticking out of a side window. He got there just in time to see three planes diving down upon them.

"Bandits!" he shouted into the intercom. "Bandits! Four o'clock high! See them?"

"Now I do," a gunner called. "I see them. Boy, what eyes, Lieutenant!"

RAT-TAT-TAT-TAT-TAT-TAT-TAT-TAT—

A hail of bullets flew out to meet the fighters. The leading plane burst into flames and exploded. The other two flipped over on their backs and started to dive out of sight.

The crew watched to see if the German fighters would return. "Guess they had enough," Lee Evans said at last. "But we still have some bombs to drop before we head for home. What about it, bombardier?"

"Steady on the target, Lee," the bombardier answered. "Straight ahead. Ready for the bomb drop."

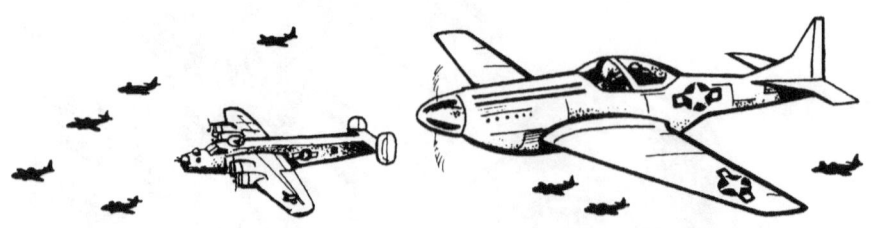

BOMBS AWAY!
CHAPTER 11

The *Screaming Eagle* was almost over the target. Mac heard the bombardier talking to Lee. "Easy, boy. I'm ready to drop our calling cards. Steady on course. Hold her level for five seconds."

"This is your show, fellow," Lee said on the intercom. "Start counting."

"Five—four—three—two—one—"

From the bomb bay came the ring of metal on metal as the bombs slipped from their racks. As they dropped through the open door the bombardier yelled, "Bombs away!"

The *Screaming Eagle*, free of her heavy load, began to climb. But Lee Evans leveled her off quickly. From far below, Mac heard the roar of the bombs as they exploded. Saw the clouds of black smoke, the flames of fire.

"Bombs away!" the bombardier yelled again. "Close bomb bay. Let's get out of here. Fast!"

"Roger," the pilot called. He tipped up the wing of the Liberator and started to make his turn. "Hey, Mac, you still back there with Andy?"

"Right," Mac answered over the intercom.

"How is our boy?"

"Pretty good. Got him patched up."

"Fine. Now get back to your table and chart us a course home."

"Roger."

Mac gave Andy a pat. "Think you can make out for a while?"

"I'm fine, sir. What about my shoulder, Lieutenant? How bad is it?"

"Give it a month and you'll be good as new."

Andy's eyes were bright above his oxygen mask. "Thanks to you, sir."

"Forget it."

Mac pushed through the bomb bay. It was empty now and its big doors were closed. He made his way along the catwalk, and crowded through the narrow doorway leading to the flight deck. He put his parachute on again and was soon back at his table. After some quick figuring he mapped out the course for Lee to follow.

"Right," Lee said. "Thanks, Mac. And say, the rest of you fellows keep your eyes open. We're still a long way from home."

No enemy fighters were spotted on the flight back to England. Looking overhead, Mac saw one good reason for it. Several groups of P-51 Mustang fighters had flown out from England to escort them safely back across the Channel.

"Boy, those Mustangs are fast babies, aren't they?" the co-pilot said. "Almost as fast as that German jet we saw a few days ago."

"Don't kid yourself," spoke up Mac. "Nothing we have is as fast as that jet. Sure, a Mustang can go, but it's still a propeller job."

"Mac's right," Lee Evans said. "That jet is in a class all its own. Let's just hope the Germans don't have many of them."

It had been a good mission. Every man had done his job, from pilot to tail gunner. This was the answer to the months of training. The months of study and drills and tests.

Enemy flak and enemy fighter planes had given them a rough time. They were no longer a green crew. They were men—fighting airmen of the Corps.

Time and again in the weeks that passed, the *Screaming Eagle* flew out on its bombing missions.

And after a short time in the hospital, Andy Mingin was back at his waist gun.

There were good missions and bad missions. Good when their bombs hit the target right on the button. Bad when they missed. Good when they got by the enemy fighters out to stop them. Good when they made it through the walls of flak. Bad when their Liberator got shot up and had to fly home on a wing and a prayer. Good to be still alive. Bad when their friends went down in flames.

One night after a hard mission Mac went to the officers' club.

He saw Lee talking to some other pilots across the room and waved to them.

"Hey, Mac," a pilot called to him. "Lee says you're the one who spotted those bandits in time to warn us. Thanks."

"Sure thing," Mac said, joining the group. "Just do the same for us some time."

Lee slapped Mac on the back. "If you weren't such a good navigator I'd make you our lookout."

"How do you do it, Mac?" someone asked. "How can you spot the enemy miles before anyone else can see them?"

"Didn't you know?" Lee cut in. "Mac has eyes like an eagle."

Mac remembered his good friend Steve Davis having said that once long ago. He wondered what had become of him. Steve hadn't answered his last letter.

"What about it, Mac? Is Lee right? Do you have eyes like an eagle?"

"An eagle—or a fighter pilot," someone else said behind them.

Mac knew that voice! He whirled around and let out a yell. "Chip! Chip Logan! What are you doing here? How? Why? Why?"

"Hey, slow down, fellow." Chip laughed as they shook hands. "I was sent over here as a fighter pilot."

"Good. But what are you doing on a bomber base?"

"I'm flying a Mustang fighter out from a field not far away. I came over to see you as soon as I heard you were here. Say, the boys tell me you knocked down one of the German planes in that big dogfight today."

Mac shook his head. "Everyone was shooting at it. We were all in on it."

"Well, that's not the way your crew is telling it. But if that's the way you want—"

"That's the way I want it," Mac said with a grin. "Let's talk about something else. Chip, have you seen any of those German jets?"

Chip laughed. "Yes, I've seen them. That is, if you can see a streak flashing past you. I tried chasing a jet one day. It flew away from me as though my Mustang were standing still."

"What I wouldn't give if we had jets like that!"

"Oh, we'll have them," Chip said. "They are starting to make a few back home. But I don't think we'll have them over here in time."

"In time?" Mac asked. "In time for what?"

"Germany can't take it much longer," Chip answered. "We're shooting down their planes faster than they can get them in the air. We're bombing their targets. The Army and Navy are—"

"That's right," spoke up another pilot. "The Allies have the upper hand now. We have almost cut off Germany's line of supplies, and without supplies no country can go on fighting. Our bomber crews have

leveled most of their factories to the ground. No factories, no machines. No machines, no war."

"It can't end too soon to suit me," Mac said. "But that means I'll end up as a navigator instead of a pilot."

Chip looked at Mac closely. "Still want to be a pilot, don't you?"

Mac nodded. "That's the way it has always been, Chip. I guess I'll always want to be a pilot—a fighter pilot."

The two friends were together a long time, laughing over their days at ground school and talking of the war. Then Chip left for his fighter base, and Mac went to his bunk and rolled in for the night.

A few more weeks passed and still Germany went on fighting. But it was a losing battle. At last, in May of 1945, Germany surrendered.

Three months later, on the far side of the world, the first atomic bomb used in any war was dropped on a city in Japan. In split seconds the city was destroyed.

Japan surrendered.

The terrible, terrible war was over. World War II was ended.

PILOT WINGS
CHAPTER 12

SOON AFTER the war ended, Mac and most of his flying friends were sent back to the United States. It was great to be back again in the country they loved. It was good to see cities where no bombs had been dropped to kill and destroy.

Now that their army flying days were over, all they talked about was going home. "I don't know what the rest of you fellows plan to do," one of them said. "But I'm getting out of this man's army just as fast as I can make it. I'll be happy to get back to my old job."

"So will I," spoke up another. "No more army life for me."

"That goes for me, too," still another said. "This flying has been great. We did it when it was needed. But I've had enough. What about you, Mac? Are you going back to your old job?"

Mac laughed a little and shook his head. "What old

job? I was just out of high school when I enlisted in the army."

"Well, don't worry. There will be plenty of jobs for all of us. Maybe I can help you get one."

"Thanks," Mac said. "But I'm staying in the Air Corps. I'm signing up for another stretch."

"Another stretch!" they shouted. "Say, what's the matter with you?"

Mac grinned. "Nothing. I joined the army to become a pilot. And that's what I'm going to be. Even though there's no war. Uncle Sam still needs pilots to keep our country from being attacked. I'm staying in until they—"

"You may be an old man."

"Then I'll be the oldest pilot in the Air Corps. But I'm staying in, anyway."

So Mac signed up for another stretch. Once again he sent in forms asking for pilot training. And once again the weeks, the months went by without an answer.

For almost two years Mac was sent from one air base to another. All the while he worked hard carrying out his orders. All the while he waited and hoped.

Then in March of 1947 Mac got the letter he knew had to come some day. His big brown hands shook as he tore it open. Quick hot tears filled his dark eyes so that he could hardly read the words. But the words were there all right. His orders to report to Randolph Field in Texas! To report for pilot training!

Mac threw back his head and shouted with sheer joy. The years of waiting, working, and dreaming had paid off.

But at the same time those very same years might also have been working against him, Mac knew. He was twenty-five years old. Not old for most things, but old to be starting training to become a fighter pilot. It would take at least a year to earn his wings.

"You'll be twenty-six, Mac," one of his friends said. "That's all right for the old prop planes. But I wouldn't try flying those new jets that the Air Force is starting to use. They're fast, Mac. Real fast. Touchy, too. And—well, they say it takes a young man to stick with them."

Mac had thought plenty about jets. Several of them had flown into the field, filled up with fuel, and whizzed off again. They were fine planes—called P-80 Shooting Stars. And they were faster than anything he had ever seen before—except once during World War II a couple of years ago.

More than anything else in the world, Mac wanted some day to be flying a jet. And now his friend was telling him he might be too old to do it.

"When I first enlisted," Mac said, "they told me I

was too young to fly. So I became a medic. Now you're trying to tell me I'm too old to make it."

"Forget it, Mac."

"I'll fly!" Mac said sharply. "And I'll fly jets. You'll see."

The weeks at Randolph Field flew by. Mac soon found that it took a lot of work and study to become a pilot. He worked and studied harder than he ever had before in his life.

"It's worth it," he said to one of his flying friends. "Worth every bit of it. When I climb into the cockpit of an airplane I'm in a different world—a wonderful world!"

"You really love to fly, don't you, Mac?"

"It's just about all I've ever wanted to do."

One day after Mac landed a small training plane, his instructor climbed out of the rear seat and jumped to the ground.

"It's all yours, Mac," he called. "Take her away."

"Alone?" Mac asked. "You mean solo?"

The instructor smiled. "Why not? You're ready to solo. You can do it, can't you?"

"Sure! Sure!"

Mac taxied the plane to the end of the runway. He called the tower for take-off instructions.

"Cleared for take-off," the tower radioed him. "Runway Two."

Mac pushed the throttle forward. "This better be good," he thought as the plane sped down the runway. "I'm on my own. No mistakes. A mistake can wash me out, or kill me."

He watched the airspeed instrument and when the speed was just right, he pulled back gently on the control stick. The plane lifted into the sky. He was so excited about his first solo that it was hard to keep his hands and feet steady on the controls. But he remembered all his lessons and all the hours of practice.

His hands grew sweaty on the control stick and they still shook a little.

"Take it easy, buddy," he told himself. "Easy. You've worked and waited a long time for this day. Now don't go and wreck your chances."

He kept talking to himself. At the same time being very careful of what he was doing with his hands and feet. Finally his hands grew steady. He stayed up for another ten minutes, trying some sharp turns.

"Hey, McConnell," the tower called, "going to stay up there all day? If so, we'll send dinner up to you."

"Coming in," Mac answered with a laugh.

"Make it good," the voice from the tower said. "Your instructor is still on the field. And he has both eyes on you."

Mac swallowed hard. He didn't need to be reminded that his instructor was watching him. Instructors always watched their students solo—watched every move they made.

Mac started down, easing back the throttle and keeping a close check on his air speed.

"So far so good," he told himself as he headed down toward the field.

"Don't go in too steeply," he told himself, seeing that he was dropping too fast. "That's it. Now keep her right there. Watch your air speed."

Then, as his wheels were almost touching the field, something went wrong. He hit the ground hard and bounced. The plane came down again on one wheel, and almost turned over. Mac finally brought it to a stop.

As the dust settled around him, Mac wiped the sweat from his face. His hands shook and his knees were weak as rags. He was sure that he would be washed out for making such a poor landing.

The instructor came racing across the field. "McConnell," he shouted, climbing up on the wing, "you're lucky to be alive. Do you know what you did wrong?"

Mac knew all right. He knew it even while the plane was bouncing high.

"I didn't check the wind, sir," Mac answered with a shake of his head.

"At least you know that much. And it was a crosswind at that. A strong gust lifted you up. then dropped you down hard. We could wash you out for making a mistake like that."

Mac didn't say anything. Was he going to be washed out on the day of his first solo?

"Don't ever forget, McConnell," the instructor went on, "you have to use your brains even more than your hands and feet when you try to fly a plane. We'll give you one more chance."

"Thank you, sir."

From then on Mac was very careful. He didn't make any more big mistakes. Before long he was as at home in the air as a bird.

One day he did some loops and some spins, and then landed as smoothly as a snowflake.

"Wow-ee!" he yelled. "This is the life."

Later that month his commanding officer sent for him. "McConnell," he said, "you've done fine so far. We're sending you on to another training base. We think you're ready to start flying a fighter plane."

"A jet?" Mac asked.

The CO smiled. "Not so fast, Lieutenant. No one jumps from small training planes right into jets. But if you do a good job in the faster prop planes, you may get your chance at the jets. You'll have to earn that chance, though. Anyway, best of luck."

"Thank you, sir."

The first day Mac arrived at the fighter training base, he went out to the flight line to look over the planes. He was walking along in front of the hangars when three jets whizzed across the field. Their wingtips seemed almost to be touching as they whistled past. At the far end of the field they zoomed up and were lost in the bright sun.

"Wow!" Mac let out a shout. "That's for me!"

When the jets were out of sight, he started looking over some of the planes standing along the flight line. He climbed up on the wing of a P-51 Mustang and looked into the cockpit. "So this is what Chip was flying in England. Not bad, but not a jet."

Down the line from the Mustangs, Mac got his first real close look at jets. There were several of them. Most were F-80s. The Air Force had recently changed the code letter for fighters from 'P' to 'F'.

"You going to be a jet pilot, Lieutenant?" a mechanic working close by asked.

"I'm sure going to give it a good try."

"They're mighty touchy, sir," the enlisted man said. "I'm a crew chief on one of those F-80s. It's hard enough for a crew chief to keep one of those babies in top flying shape all the time. But the pilots—well, they have the real job."

"A pilot is never better than his plane," Mac said. "You crew chiefs have a real job, too."

"Thanks, sir," the man said, smiling proudly.

"Anyway, some of the pilots say that they can hardly think fast enough to keep up with the plane. Those jets are so fast that by the time the pilot figures out what to do next it's too late to do it."

"Guess the only answer is to think faster."

"That's the answer, sir," the mechanic nodded. "Those who can, become jet pilots. Those who can't—"

"I'll remember that," Mac said. "Thanks."

At the end of the line there were a couple F-84 Thunderjets, the newest and hottest jet fighters made in the United States. There had been much talk about still another fighter jet. It was even faster than the Thunderjet. Its wings were swept back sharply, and it was called the F-86 Sabre. But so far Mac had only seen pictures of the Sabre.

After looking over the jets, Mac started back toward the officers' club. A mechanic came out of a hangar and headed across the field.

That walk—that back—Mac was sure he had seen them before…many times. Then the fellow stopped and turned to glance up at a plane coming in for a landing. Mac got a look at him and he saw the thick horn-rimmed glasses, the thin, friendly face.

"Steve!" he yelled. "Steve Davis!"

The mechanic turned around. Behind his thick glasses his blue eyes opened wide in surprise.

"Mac!" he shouted. "Joe McConnell! Of all—"

Steve stopped and stood at attention. "It's mighty good to see you, sir."

"Forget that 'sir' stuff!" Mac threw his arm around Steve's shoulder.

"Hey, watch the rules, Mac. You're an officer. I'm an enlisted man. The rules say—"

"Sure, sure. I know the rules, pal," Mac said. "But we're old friends. Hey, what are you doing here? How long have you been in this man's Air Force?"

"I joined it way back when it was still called the Army Air Corps," Steve answered. "Right after I was graduated from high school. After basic training I was sent to a mechanics' school."

"You always were a whiz with engines and things, Steve."

"I like it, Mac, and I guess Uncle Sam likes my work, too. I was made sergeant about a year ago. Then they sent me here—just where I want to be."

"Why here?"

"Jet engines, Mac. This is pretty much of a jet base. There are still some prop planes. But before long it will be all jets. And I'm working with jet engines."

"Wow!" Mac exclaimed. "You've really gone to town, Steve. That's great. I'm sure proud of you."

Steve's face turned red. "Hey, cut that out. Now, how about telling me what you're doing here?"

"Training to be a fighter pilot."

"I'm glad, Mac. You always wanted to be a pilot. It has been a long time coming, hasn't it?"

"Sure has," Mac said. "But I guess the best things take the longest time. Hey, Steve, is there any chance of your being my crew chief? I'd sure like to have you taking care of my jet."

"I'd like that too, Mac. But you won't be flying jets right away. They'll start you out in Mustangs. And, well, my CO doesn't want me working on prop engines. He thinks I'm a jet man."

"OK," Mac said. "But when I start flying jets, maybe I'll be lucky enough to have you as crew chief."

"You know the Air Force. A fellow doesn't always get to do just what he wants."

"Don't I know it," Mac said, thinking of how long it had taken him to become a pilot. And he wasn't finished yet.

"But when the time comes, I'll sure try to be signed to your plane. OK?"

Steve, his face suddenly serious, went on. "Be careful, Mac. It's a rough job being a fighter pilot. I've seen a lot of them get washed out."

"I'll watch it," Mac said. "And thanks, pal. And now I better go get my things put away. I'm going to start flying Mustangs tomorrow."

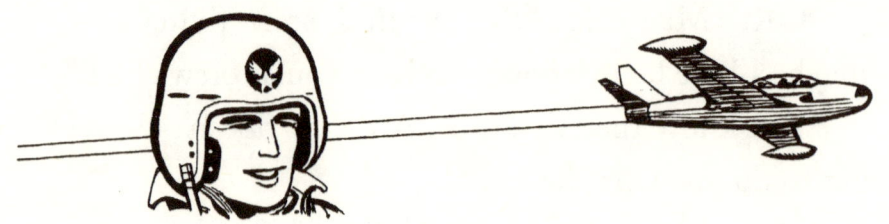

THE TIGER ROARS
CHAPTER 13

The Mustang was a hard plane to fly. It was nearly twice as fast as anything Mac had flown before. And it was touchy, real touchy. Once when he forgot to move the controls gently, the plane began to buck all over the sky.

"Whoa!" Mac yelled, just as he might to a bucking mustang. "Whoa!"

When he had the plane under control again, he laughed to himself, "Boy, I'll have to watch out! This plane is full of tricks."

But Mac was a good flier. Before long he knew all the tricks of the fast little Mustang.

One day while he was flying he did a couple loops high in the air. Then he zoomed down low across the field. He pushed the throttle forward and roared in low at full speed. He did a couple slow rolls, then leveled off. At the end of the field Mac pulled the throttle back to

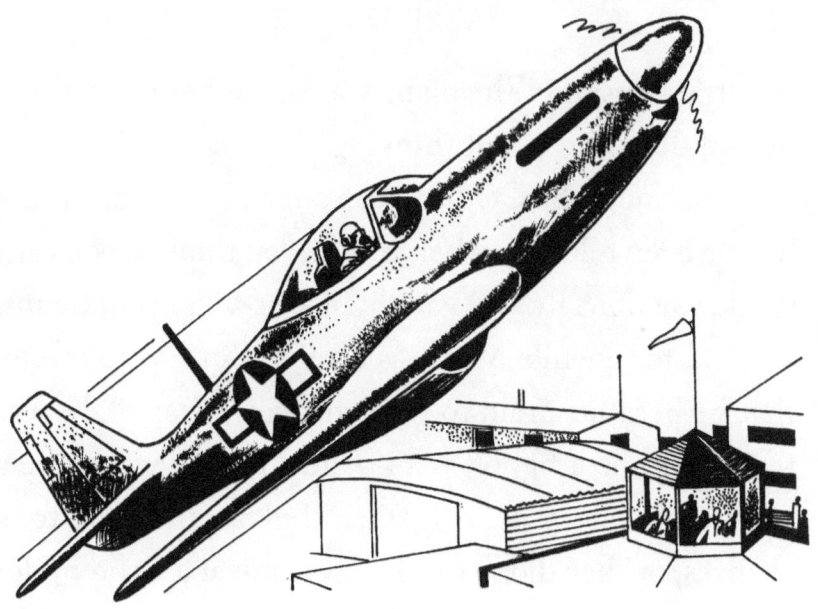

slow his speed. He made his turn around the field and came in to land.

The CO was waiting as Mac climbed out of the plane. One look at the officer's angry face and Mac knew he was in trouble.

"McConnell," the CO said in an angry voice, "pull another trick like those low altitude rolls and I'll wash you out. Just like that!" The CO snapped his fingers. "Is that clear?"

"Yes, sir."

Mac knew he had it coming. Rolling a plane close to the ground was crazy. It was one thing to be brave, quite another to take chances just for fun. Had anything happened to the plane he could have crashed to his death.

But up in the sky he had been so sure of himself and

his little Mustang. The plane was so easy to handle that he had done it without thinking.

No wonder the CO had been angry. How many times had he been told that when you fly, you think. If you can't think, you don't fly. Use your brains, boy. Use your brains.

And for a while Mac was careful. But not so careful that he became afraid to take chances. After all, he was training to be a fighter pilot. And the only way to be a good one was to be a tiger, as they said. Tigers took chances, or they didn't eat. In time of war a fighter pilot had to be like a tiger. He had to get the jump on the enemy first. Then move in fast for the kill—or be killed.

Mac soon finished his training in the Mustangs. Now there was only one kind of plane left for him to fly. It was the plane he had dreamed of flying.

A jet!

"McConnell," his commander asked, "do you think you are tiger enough to fly a jet?"

In answer Mac roared like a tiger.

The squadron CO laughed. "You're ready. Tomorrow you start with the F-80s."

"Thank you, sir!"

"Don't thank me, Mac. You earned it."

For several days Mac "flew the books." He studied all there was to know about flying jets. He went to classes and heard jet pilots with many hours of flying time tell how jets were different from prop planes. He learned to use the many new instruments.

"Just remember," a jet pilot told him, "that jets are even more touchy than the Mustangs. Go real easy on the controls. And the jets are faster than anything else in the sky. That means you have to think faster."

Hour after hour Mac sat in the cockpit of an F-80 going through all the steps of flying without leaving the ground. An instructor stood on the wing, leaning over him and watching every move.

Mac learned how to use the ejection seat. In case of trouble he was to squeeze a trigger under the arm rest of his seat. This would shoot him away from the plane. Once free from the plane, he could pull the ripcord of his parachute and float safely down to the ground.

Day after day Mac went over the lessons with his instructor. At last the time came when the instructor said, "All right, Mac. You're ready to take her up. Come on, let's go."

Mac wanted to shout with joy. But instead he roared like a tiger—a very big tiger. Then he followed the instructor to the flight line where his F-80 was waiting for him. And standing beside the Shooting Star was Steve Davis.

"Hi, there," Mac greeted his friend. "How did you know I was flying today?"

"What do you mean, how did I know?" Steve asked with a smile. "I'm your crew chief."

"Wow! That's great. What luck."

"She's all checked out and full of fuel," Steve said. "She's ready. But let's see if you can find anything wrong."

Mac walked around the plane, looking carefully for anything that was out of order. He moved the rudder to see that it worked freely. He tapped the extra fuel tanks hanging under each wing and nodded as the sound told him they were full.

Those extra wing tanks were not too important here in training. In combat, though, they would be very important, adding many miles to the jet's range. But the wing tanks did slow a plane down quite a bit. One of the first lessons Mac had learned was that a pilot always dropped the wing tanks before going into combat. And that was done simply by pulling a handle in the cockpit.

Mac finished his check. Just as he expected, he found nothing wrong. But it was a rule that every pilot must make his own check of the plane before take-off.

"Everything's fine, Steve," he said. "OK, let's go." He climbed into the cockpit, pulled on his crash helmet, and strapped himself in.

The instructor climbed up on the wing. He leaned over Mac and began asking a hundred questions. Mac answered them one by one.

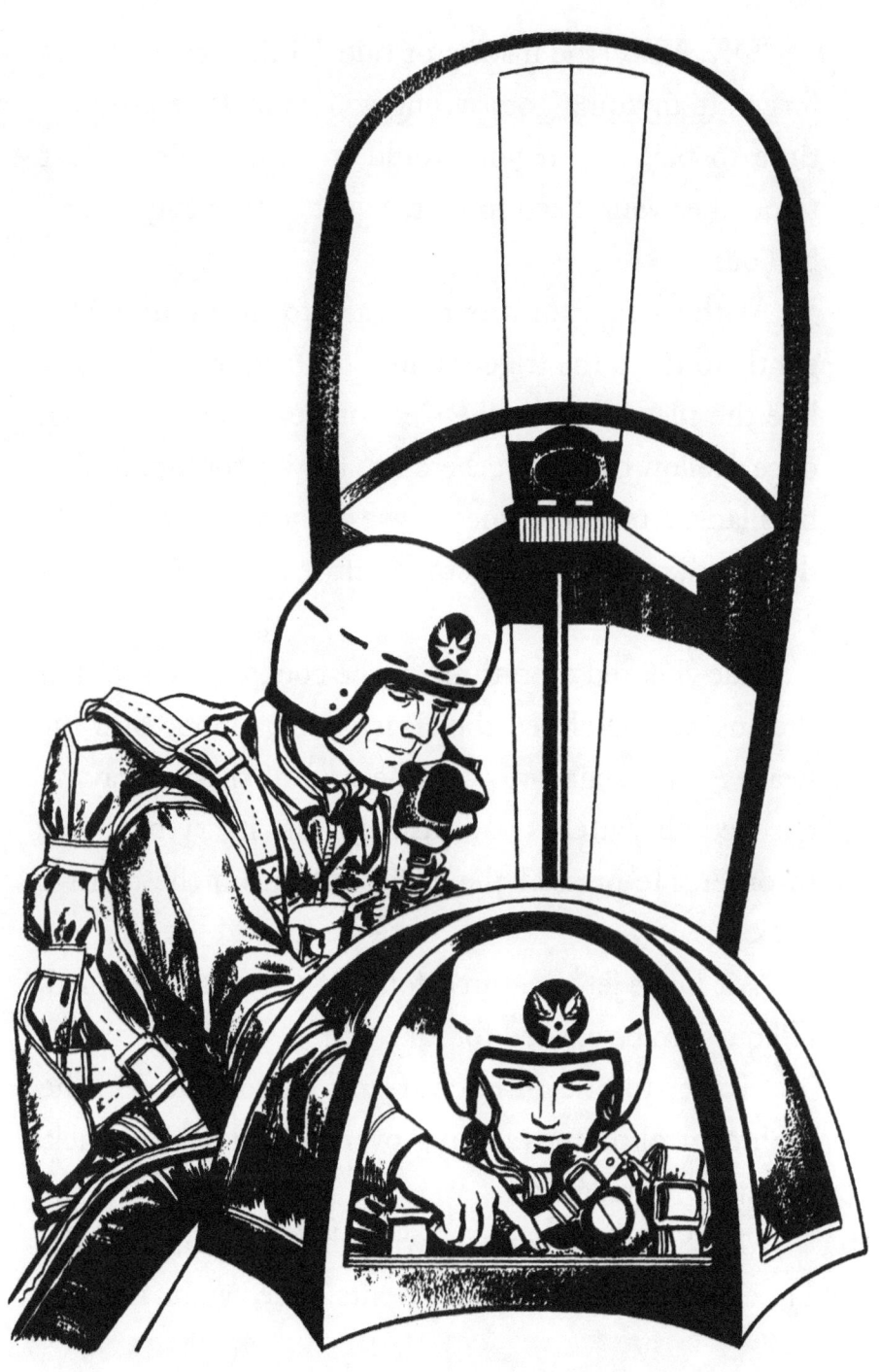

"OK, Mac," the instructor said. "Take her up. Don't forget, if anything goes wrong you won't have as much time to bail out as you would in a prop plane. Just remember your ejection seat. Squeeze that trigger and bail out."

As the instructor dropped back to the ground Mac gently touched the trigger under the arm rest. He didn't like the idea of using the ejection seat. For one thing, once a fellow bailed out there was no way for him to save his plane. And sometimes, if the plane wasn't too badly damaged, a pilot could stay with it and keep it from crashing.

Mac checked everything in the cockpit, then started the engine. He closed the clear plastic canopy over his head. As he taxied toward the end of the runway he checked all switches and instruments. Everything was in order. He pressed the radio button on the control stick.

"Air Force jet one-three-four-six to tower," he called. "Request to be cleared for take-off."

"Tower to one-three-four-six," the operator in the high control room watching over the field called back. "Cleared for take-off."

Mac lined his plane up with the long runway strip. He checked over his instruments once again. Then he reached with his left hand and pushed the throttle forward.

The whine of the jet engine grew louder and louder until it became a roar. The plane started forward, picking up speed.

Mac kept checking his instruments and watching the runway ahead. The plane raced along. When the speed was right, Mac pulled back gently on the control stick.

The jet lifted smoothly into the sky. Mac shouted with joy.

"Hey, cut it out, McConnell!" a voice called over the radio.

Mac suddenly remembered that his own radio mike was on. He probably had blasted the tower operator's ears with the shout. He smiled to himself. Nothing could bother him now.

But something did!

He had been in the air for about half an hour when it happened. He was just getting used to the feel of the controls, to the soft whine of the jet engine, when it happened.

Without any warning the engine stopped. A red light began to flash in front of him. The hands of some instruments swung around to zero.

The red warning light and the instruments showed what was wrong. Flame-out! The fire had gone out in the jet engine. And without fire there was no power.

A chill ran down Mac's back. All jet pilots worry about a flame-out. And now, on his very first flight, Mac had one!

Without power, the plane began dropping fast. Mac glanced over the side. The ground seemed to be rushing up toward him.

"I've flamed out!" Mac called into his radio.

"What's your altitude, McConnell?" the voice from the control tower came back at once.

"Eight thousand," Mac reported, reading his altimeter.

"Try one restart, McConnell," the voice said again. "If it doesn't work, bail out. Get out of that plane before you drop below fifteen hundred feet. Understand?"

But Mac was too busy to answer. He thought of all the things he had learned about restarting a flamed-out jet engine.

He began doing them, one by one.

But the engine would not restart.

"Bail out, McConnell!"

"One more try," Mac called out, more to himself than to the tower operator. "One more try."

Quickly he went through the steps. Step by step.

"Watch your instruments," he told himself. "Give it some fuel. Easy now. Ready with the switch."

Suddenly, as he flipped the switch, the engine burst into a roar. The red warning light stopped flashing. The hands of the instruments swung back from zero.

"It worked!" he shouted. "I made it work!"

"Good boy," the voice from the tower came in again. "But stop shouting. I need my ears. By the way, what's your altitude?"

Mac took a quick look at the altimeter. "A—a little under a thousand feet, but I'm climbing—"

The tower operator cut in with a long soft whistle. "Mac, you don't know how lucky you are. If that engine hadn't started and you had bailed out that low, you might have hit the ground before your parachute had a chance to open."

Mac knew he was right. The thought left an empty feeling inside of him.

But the tower operator was saying something. "Mac, if I were you I'd keep right on flying."

"Why?"

"You were told to bail out. Remember? Your instructor is waiting for you to land. And boy, is he burned up. You're in for it. But in my book you're all right, Mac. You're a tiger!"

TEN FEET TALL
CHAPTER 14

MAC STOOD at attention beside the plane while the hot words of the instructor tore at him.

"McConnell," the instructor demanded, "didn't you hear that order to bail out?"

"Yes, sir."

"Then why didn't you bail out?"

"I was trying to restart the engine and—"

"Sometimes I think that if we washed you out we'd be saving a lot of people a lot of trouble. You sure pull some fine stunts, Mac. You know that, don't you?"

"Yes, sir," Mac answered. He didn't try to get out of it. Besides, orders were orders. And no matter what the reason, he had failed to obey one. For that one mistake his pilot days might be over. He was sick inside about it.

"Mac, I'll have to report this to the CO," the instructor went on. Then he smiled. "But I'll also put in a word for you. You may have made a mistake, but you have all the makings of a tiger. And that's what we want around here."

Mac could hardly believe his ears. His instructor was a real good Joe. "Thank you, sir. Thank you."

"Just watch yourself, Mac."

"I will. I will, sir."

"What you did was wrong, McConnell," the instructor went on. "At the same time, you saved a very valuable jet. But after this, orders come first. That's all, Lieutenant."

In the days that followed, Mac took many more flights in the F-80. He made some mistakes, but not big ones. And each day he was better at the controls. Before long he felt as though he were part of the plane. The weeks, the months of training went on and on. At last Mac and a few others were graduated, one of the first classes specially trained as jet fighters.

Mac, looking at his new silver wings, couldn't help feeling ten feet tall. Once he had been told that he was too young to join the Air Corps. Then he was told he was too old to fly jets. Too young, too old. Maybe so. But he had never given up and now he had his wings—the wings of a jet fighter pilot. A fighter pilot in the United States Air Force!

A few weeks after getting his wings, Mac was sent to another air base for gunnery training. No matter how well he could fly, he wasn't a real fighter pilot until he was a sharp-shooter, too. No matter how well he handled his plane, he had to handle his machine guns as well.

After all, fighter pilots were fighters. In a war it was their job to get control of the air. Win control and keep it. And that meant shooting down the planes of the enemy.

During the first briefing at gunnery school, the pilots were told that part of their training would be learning to fly in pairs. Each pair would be made up of a leader and a wingman who would fly a little behind the leader.

"In war time the lead pilot does most of the fighting," the instructor said. "The wingman's job is to protect the leader. Now I suppose each of you will want to be a leader. Well, remember this, you have to earn that position. Be a good wingman and in time you'll be made the leader of an element. Who knows what an element is?"

"An element is two fighter planes, sir. Leader and wingman."

"Right. And a flight?"

"Two elements. Four planes."

"Right. To go on, there are also two to four flights in a squadron. Several squadrons make up a group, and—"

There was more to learn—lots more. But the most important idea the instructor put across was that there were no lone tiger fighter pilots. It was all a matter of close teamwork between wingman and leader. And this teamwork spread out between elements and flights and squadrons.

Teamwork. Teamwork. Teamwork had been a big part of Mac's training ever since he had enlisted in the army.

And teamwork was still with him here in gunnery school. Plenty of it. He and the other pilot of his element took turns when they flew out on their gunnery practice flights. One day Mac would be the wingman. The next day he would be the leader.

On the practice flights the leader of each element shot at a target being pulled on a long wire behind another plane.

Gunnery practice was hard work, calling for steady nerves and quick thinking on the part of a fighter pilot. Hard work to fly a fast little jet and at the same time line up the orange-colored target in your gun sights and fire before it was gone.

Once when Mac was flying the lead he caught sight of the orange target.

"Red Leader to wingman," Mac called over his radio. "There goes a bandit—ten o'clock low!"

"Get it, Red Leader," came his wingman's answer. "I'm right with you."

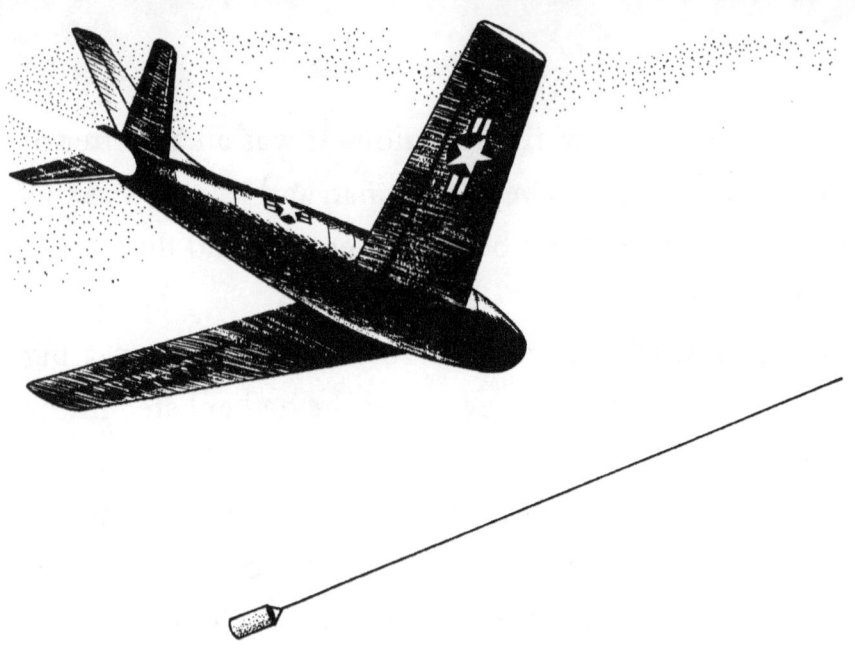

They banked together to the left and dived down at the orange target. Mac turned sharply, trying to get the fast moving target in his gun sights.

He tried again and then he had it. Right in the middle of his sights. Quickly he pressed the gun button on the control stick.

RAT-TAT-TAT-TAT-TAT-TAT-TAT-TAT—

The machine-gun bullets with tracers trailing smoke streaked toward the target.

"You got it, Mac!" his wingman called. "Good shooting, boy."

"OK, I'll take the wing spot now," Mac called back. "Let's see what you can do."

It went that way day after day. And each day more bullets hit the target.

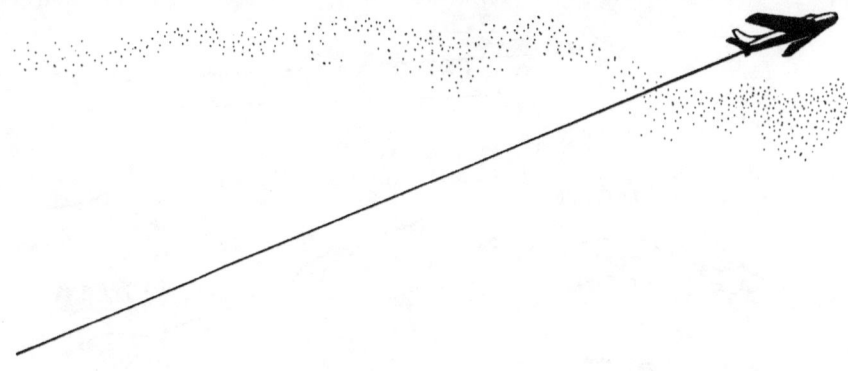

"You're getting to be a real eagle-eye, Mac," his squadron commander told him. "Keep it up."

Practice, practice, and more practice. Weeks, months, years passed. Mac was sent from one air base to another. Much of the time was spent flying patrols in late model jets.

"We have to keep a careful watch," he was told. "One of these days the Commies may try to take over all Korea. They have no right to do this. We must be ready in case the Commies get any big ideas about starting a war."

Still more time passed. Mac was sent to other bases. He finally ended up in Alaska, where he flew fighter patrols out over land and sea.

Then, on June 25, 1950, the war in Korea started.

When World War II ended in 1945, Korea, a finger of land sticking out into the sea near Japan, had been cut in half. The Communists had taken over the north half. The free Koreans had stayed in the south half.

And now the communists were trying to take over all of Korea.

"It's a war!" one of Mac's pilot friends shouted, waving a paper with the big headlines

COMMUNISTS ATTACK SOUTH KOREA

"That's right," Mac agreed. "It will be a job for the United Nations to help the South Koreans keep their freedom."

"We're part of the United Nations," his friend said. "So if this is war, then we're in it, too."

"That's right. As a member of the UN, the United States must help protect any country that is attacked by another."

"You think we'll be sent over to Korea?"

"I hope so," Mac answered quickly. "I'm all for jumping in to help those South Koreans. If the Communists get away with this, they'll try it again and again with other countries. They'll keep on killing and—"

"We can't let them do that! The Communists will try to take over the whole world!"

"That's right," Mac said. "And I'm going to ask to be sent to Korea to help stop them."

But Mac found it wasn't that easy. He was needed to fly patrols in the far north. He was kept in Alaska for another year. Then he was called back to the United States for still another year of duty.

And all this time the war raged on in Korea. By now Mac was afraid he would never get there. He was thirty years old. Most of the fighter pilots being sent there were much younger.

"Boy, this is a fine thing," Mac said one day to his friends in the barracks. "I've spent the last twelve years of my life trying to become a fighter pilot. And now they seem to think I'm too old to fight."

It was a bitter pill to swallow. But Mac wasn't one to give up. He kept asking for duty in Korea.

"Wait a little longer," he was told.

Wait. Wait. Wait. Mac was sick of waiting.

Then one day his orders came through.

"Wow-ee!" Mac yelled. "I made it! I finally made it!"

KOREA
CHAPTER 15

A FEW DAYS later Mac was on a big transport plane heading for Japan. As soon as the plane landed, Mac reported to the officer in command of the new pilots arriving from the United States.

"Lieutenant McConnell," the officer said, running his finger down a list of names. "Oh, yes, here you are. You're going to K-13."

"That's right," Mac said, showing his orders to the officer. "I believe it's near Suwon."

"Right you are, Lieutenant. Suwon Air Base—code number K-13. You're to join the 51st Fighter Group. If you're looking for action, McConnell, you'll get it with the 51st. They're as fighting a bunch of tigers as you'll find in all Korea."

"Great," Mac said. "I'm over here to fight."

"There's a plane taking off for Korea at eight in the morning. You be here to catch it."

"Yes, sir," Mac said, picking up his bag. "See you at eight in the morning."

In the morning Mac and a few other fliers were on the plane flying across the narrow Sea of Japan to Korea.

"You reporting for duty at Suwon, too?" Mac asked a young pilot seated next to him.

"No," the officer answered. "I'm joining a fighter squadron based at Kimpo. By the way, I'm Pete." The pilot held out his hand. His dark eyes were bright and friendly.

"I'm Mac." They shook hands.

"Tell you what, Mac, I'll bet you a dinner—all you can eat, that I shoot down more MIGs than you."

"You're on," Mac said. "It's a bet. And you better save your money. I can eat plenty when it's free."

They laughed. Then the plane made its landing at Kimpo, letting off Pete and several of the other pilots. Soon it took off again, flying south toward Suwon. As the plane circled for a landing, Mac looked down and saw the air base lying in a valley. Great long hangars lined the runway. The control tower at one side of the runway stood taller than any other building. A short distance back from the runway were the barracks where the officers and enlisted men lived.

After the plane touched down and rolled to a stop,

Mac and the other fliers climbed out. It was a clear summer day, but already there was a chill in the August air.

Mac looked around at the silver swept-winged F-86 Sabre jets parked along the flight line.

"I wonder which one of those babies I'll fly?" Mac asked.

"You'll find out soon enough," an officer who was there to meet the new pilots said. "But first you men better put your stuff away and report for a briefing. I'll meet you here in fifteen minutes and take you there."

In less than ten minutes Mac had put his things in the barracks and hurried back. The others arrived shortly after. They fell into step with the officer, who led them to a building where the briefing was to take place.

Several other pilots were already in the room by the time Mac and his friends arrived. And the first pilot Mac saw as he walked into the room had red hair.

"Chip!" he shouted. "Chip Logan!"

"Quiet!" an officer commanded. "The briefing comes first. There will be time later for any of you new men to greet your buddies."

Mac felt his face get hot as the others turned and grinned at him. He sat down in a chair beside Chip. His friend looked at him as though to say, "Later, Mac. Later."

"Attention!"

All the pilots jumped to their feet as the group commander hurried into the briefing room.

"As you were, men," the colonel said when he

reached the front of the room and turned to face them. "First, I want to welcome you new men," the CO went on. "This is it, boys. This is the end of the line. This is what you have been training for—and you'll find out how well you have been trained. Two things happen over here, you get shot at and you shoot. But the pilot who has trained properly will do more shooting and get shot at less."

There were a few laughs.

"Most of you know what this war is all about by now. But let's just go over it quickly. As a member nation of the UN, it is our duty to keep the Communists out of South Korea. The Commies nearly ran us into the sea a couple of years ago, but we pushed them back. They would like to do it again. Run us all the way out and make all of Korea a Communist country. We're not going to let them!

"That's the big picture. Our own part of the picture —our job here at K-13—is to shoot down all the MIGs we can. We must control the sky. If we can control the sky, we can control the ground beneath it. If the Air Force can take care of the air, the Army and Navy will take care of the rest."

"We'll do it," one of the new pilots cried. "We'll do it!"

The colonel smiled. "You bet we will! But it won't

be an easy job. The Commie pilots in North Korea have some of the hottest planes in the sky."

"MIG-15s?" someone asked.

"That's right. And don't kid yourselves. Those MIGs are good planes. Real good planes. They can fly faster and climb faster than anything the UN has in the air."

Mac wondered if the MIGs could fly faster and climb faster than the F-86 Sabre jets.

"They can even fly faster and climb faster than our Sabres," the colonel went on as though reading Mac's mind. "But our pilots are better than the Red pilots. We're better trained, and we're fighting for something very important—freedom for the South Koreans. They're a fine and friendly people. But they need help. The United States and other UN countries are giving them that help. Just don't get the idea that this is a game. It's a war. A big war. And we must win it."

The CO then got down to the real business at hand.

"You know from your training what our combat setup is here," he said. "Our basic flight is four planes…made up of two elements…two leaders and two wingmen. The flight leader is Number One man. His wingman is Number Two. The leader of the other element is Number Three. His wingman is Number Four. It's that simple. The best thing to do is to keep the flight together at all times. But this is not always possible. If you get into a dogfight with a bunch of MIGs you often get split up. OK, you can't very well help that. But if you do get split up into elements, remember one thing. The wingman always sticks with his leader. Always! Don't any of you wingmen ever leave your leader alone. If I ever hear of such a case you'll never become a leader yourself—not as long as I'm CO of this group."

Mac could tell that the colonel meant what he said. Mac had learned from his training days how important it was for the wingman to stay close to his leader.

"Of course, all you new men will start out as wingmen," the CO said. "How soon you become leaders will be pretty much up to you. One thing is sure—you will have to earn it. Well! That's about it for this time. Now to place you in your squadrons."

He turned to an officer standing near by. "Take over."

Mac waited for his name to be called.

"...McConnell, Jr., Joseph...39th Fighter Squadron..."

"Mac," Chip said, grinning, "that's Cobra Squadron. My squadron."

"Great," Mac said. "Great! Then we're together." The way his friend was smiling, Mac had an idea that Chip might have had something to do with his being placed with the 39th.

When the briefing broke up, Mac and Chip were free to spend the rest of the day together. Years had passed since they had last seen each other. There was much to talk about. Most of their talk was about flying and jets.

"Are the MIGs really as good as the colonel said?" Mac asked.

"They are, Mac. Every bit as good."

"That's hard to believe," Mac said. "But you've been over here long enough to know."

"I know all right. And those MIG pilots can shoot, too. I found out."

"Found out? How?"

All at once Chip was serious. He turned his head so that Mac got a look at the other side of his friend's face.

A rough, red scar ran from the side of Chip's jaw down along his neck. It was the kind of scar that a bullet might make.

Chip smiled at him. "It doesn't hurt, Mac. Not now, anyway. But just don't let it happen to you!"

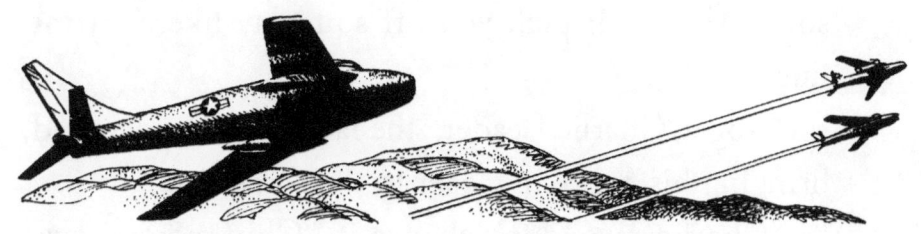

MIG ALLEY
CHAPTER 16

Mac's second bit of luck—and another thing with which Chip might have had something to do—was being made a member of Charlie Flight. Chip was leader of Charlie Flight.

For the first week or two the flight flew practice missions to show Mac and the other new wingmen their duties and to build flight teamwork.

Chip pushed them hard, trying to get them ready for battle as quickly as possible. He knew what he was doing. Chip hadn't talked much about it, but Mac knew that his friend had been in some big dogfights with MIG planes. The two small red stars painted on the side of Chip's cockpit showed that he already had shot down two enemy planes.

"Charlie Leader to Charlie Four," Chip called on his radio during a practice mission. "You're too far out of formation. Come in closer. If you stay way out there some MIG will pick you off someday like a sitting duck."

"Roger, Charlie Leader," the far wingman answered, bringing his Sabre in closer to the formation.

"Charlie Two, don't chance it," Chip radioed over to Mac. "I like to have my wingman stick close, Mac. But don't make it so close that you scratch my wings."

Mac smiled to himself behind his oxygen mask. He had been sticking so close to Chip's plane that he could read the small letters on its side. Now he dropped a little farther back and to the side.

"We're doing fine now," Chip called. "Later, when we go into battle, try to keep it this way. But if the flight has to break up into two elements, Mac, you stay with me. Charlie Four, you stick with your leader, Charlie Three. And whatever you do, don't lose him. Understand?"

"Roger."

It went that way, day after day. Practice, practice, and more practice. Each day the men proudly tied on the bright yellow scarf which marked them as members of Cobra Squadron.

"Chip, when are we going to get our chance at some MIGs?" Mac asked one day.

Chip smiled. "Getting in a hurry, are you, Mac? Well, don't worry, it could be any time now. I told the squadron CO today that Charlie Flight is ready for combat."

In the morning the command was given that Mac had been waiting for since landing in Korea.

"Cobra Squadron—all flights—report at once for combat briefing. Repeat. All flights. Cobra Squadron, report at once for combat briefing!"

Mac put away the letter he had been writing to his folks at home. He pulled on his flight suit and tied the yellow scarf around his neck.

"This is it," he said as he strapped on his Mae West.

"Right," Chip answered. "Let's go get us some MIGs."

The men of Charlie Flight were first to reach the briefing room. They were followed closely by the pilots of the other three flights which rounded out the squadron.

"All right, men," the squadron commander said, looking around the room. "Your mission this morning is a simple one. Fly up to MIG Alley and try to bag yourself some MIGs."

Mac let out a shout.

The CO looked at him sharply, then smiled. "Easy, McConnell. And don't forget that you're a wingman. Stick to your leader. Protect him at all times. Let him do the shooting."

"Yes, sir," Mac said.

"Good. And that goes for the rest of you wingmen," the CO went on. "At times when the setup is just right, your leader may tell you to break off and take out after a MIG. But wait until your leader tells you."

Mac wondered if he would get such a chance to go after his own MIG. He hoped so.

"I'll remind you flight leaders," the squadron commander said, "to have your men test their guns before going into battle. A short burst is enough. If anybody's gun jams, head for home. You're no good up there if you can't shoot. Second, before you go into battle, be sure to drop your wing tanks. You'll need all the extra speed you can get against those MIGs.

"Oh, yes, just one other thing. Don't forget the standing order of this war. You cannot cross the Yalu River to the far side. It's against rules. If you are chasing a MIG and it runs to the far side of the Yalu, let it go."

It was a strange order, Mac thought. But it was an order, and every UN pilot obeyed it, if he liked it or not.

When the briefing was over, the pilots went out to their planes. As they hurried down the flight line Chip spoke a few last words to the other three members of Charlie Flight.

"Let's keep off the radio as much as possible," Chip said. "Keep from tipping off the Reds that we're around. But if we get separated, or you get into trouble, use your radio to call for help. And use it fast. OK, let's go."

As Mac reached his waiting Sabre he stopped cold. A lone figure was standing beside the plane, grinning at him.

"Steve Davis! What are you doing here, pal?"

"Why, Mac," Steve said, his eyes shining. "You didn't think I could let you come over here and fight the war without me, did you?"

"You mean—"

"I'm your new crew chief," Steve said, grinning proudly from ear to ear.

"Great!" Mac cried. "How lucky can I get?"

"Luck, my eye," his tall, skinny friend said. "I've been over at another air base for nearly a year. When I heard you were here at K-13 I asked to be sent over. It wasn't easy, but I made it."

"I still say I'm lucky," Mac said. "My two best friends are here. You and Chip Logan."

"Yes, I've seen him," Steve said. "But right now we better get this plane fired up, Mac. You don't want to get left behind on your first combat mission, do you?"

"I'll say not. Let's go." Mac climbed up the side of the plane and let himself down into the Sabre's little cockpit.

All around him jet engines began to come to life. Soon the planes began to take off in elements of two. Once they had enough altitude they joined their flights, then turned north and flew toward the Yalu River…and MIG Alley. They tested their guns, then settled down for the two hundred mile trip to MIG Alley.

The planes of Charlie Flight kept radio silence as they flew north. Mac stuck close to Chip's side. Glancing down now and then, he saw the green wooded hills and the valleys turning brown as winter drew near.

As yet, Mac had seen little of Korea, except from the air. But what little he had seen he liked. The people were friendly and they worked hard. Even with a terrible war going on around them, they were brave and carried on with high spirits.

Soon the squadron had crossed into North Korea. Enemy territory.

"From up here it looks about the same as South Korea," Mac told himself. "But I wouldn't want to get shot up and have to bail out and land down there. Those Commies are plenty rough on anyone they can take alive."

Before long Mac saw a winding yellow river. He checked his map. It was the Yalu River, all right.

"We must be in MIG Alley," he said to himself.

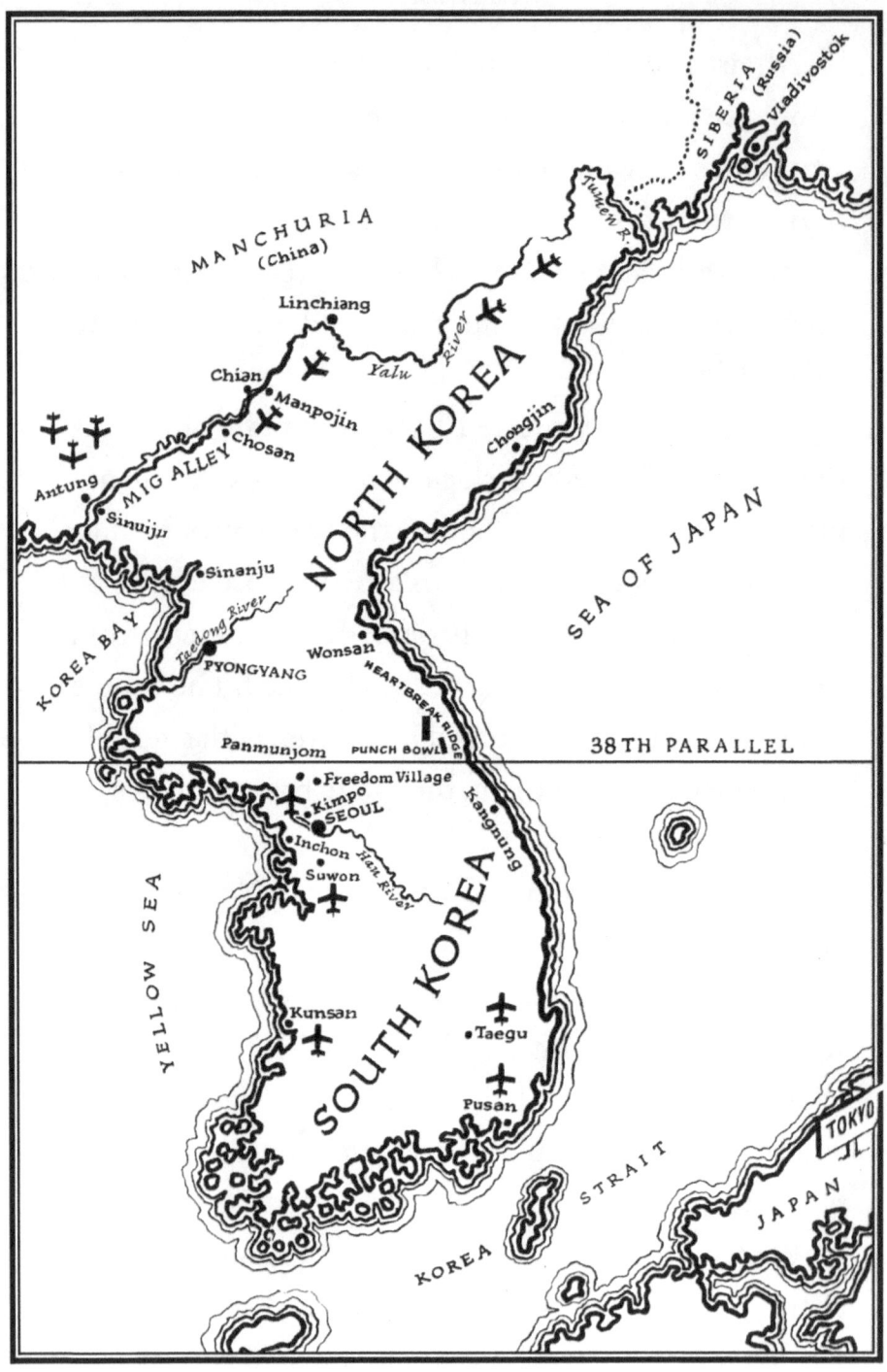

He glanced toward Chip's Sabre. Chip turned in his cockpit. He pointed down and nodded, as though knowing what Mac was thinking.

The four planes turned east and started flying along MIG Alley. Except for the other flights of Cobra Squadron off in the distance, there didn't seem to be a thing in the sky. A half hour passed.

"This is not our day," Chip radioed after Charlie Four had reported that his fuel was getting low. "Let's head back for K-13 and—"

"Wingman to Charlie Leader," Mac cut in suddenly on the radio. "Bandits straight ahead! Twelve o'clock high!"

"You sure, Mac? I don't see them."

"Twelve o'clock high! Six of them!"

"I see them now," Charlie Four's words came over the air. "What eyes, Mac. What eyes!"

"See them, Chip?" Mac asked.

"I've got them now, Mac. How's your fuel, Charlie Four?"

"Low, but enough for at least one pass at them," the far wingman answered.

"OK, Charlie Flight. Drop your wing tanks. Let's go!"

Mac pulled a handle and felt his plane shoot ahead as his wing tanks dropped away. He pushed his throttle full forward to keep up with Chip's speeding Sabre. In tight formation the four planes of Charlie Flight climbed toward the six dots in the sky.

As they drew closer, Chip broke radio silence again. "They're MIGs, all right," he called. "But they see us. Look at them go!"

"They're running away," Mac called. "Let's get them!"

"Hold it, Charlie Flight," Chip radioed quickly. "They're faster than we are. And they're already crossing the Yalu."

"Running away! Those Commies…those Reds… they're running away!"

"There are six of them to four of us. And still they're running away!"

"Doesn't seem they want to fight," Chip's voice came again. "Well, we can't catch them now. And we can't chase them across the Yalu. You know the order."

Mac felt a little sick. Here was his first chance for combat, and the Reds had turned tail and raced away.

"Leader to Charlie Flight," Chip's voice on the radio was firm. "Back we go to Suwon. Better hunting another day. Breaking right—now!"

At the warning command Chip banked sharply to the right. Mac and the other Charlie Flight Sabres banked with their leader, keeping their tight formation

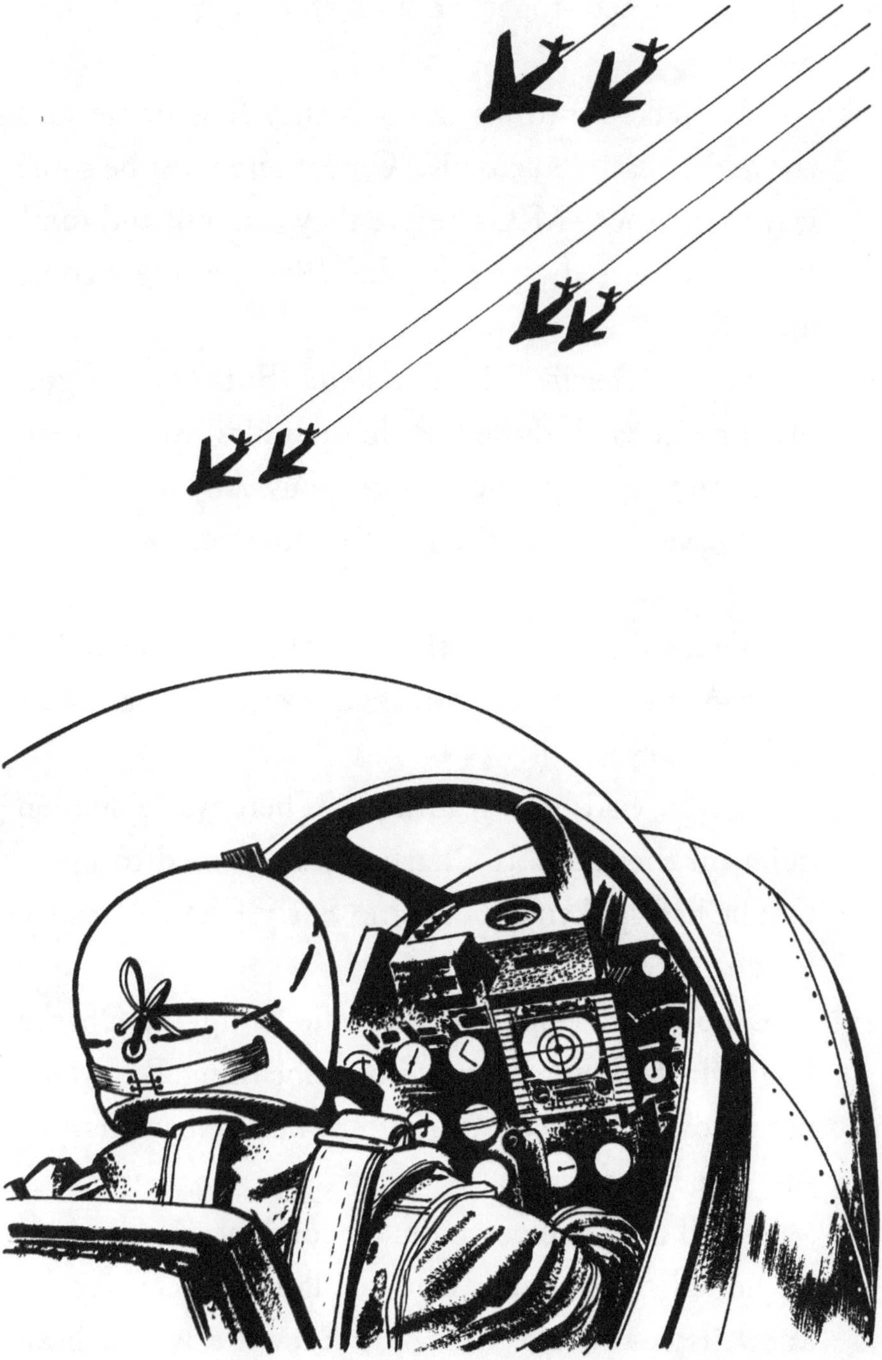

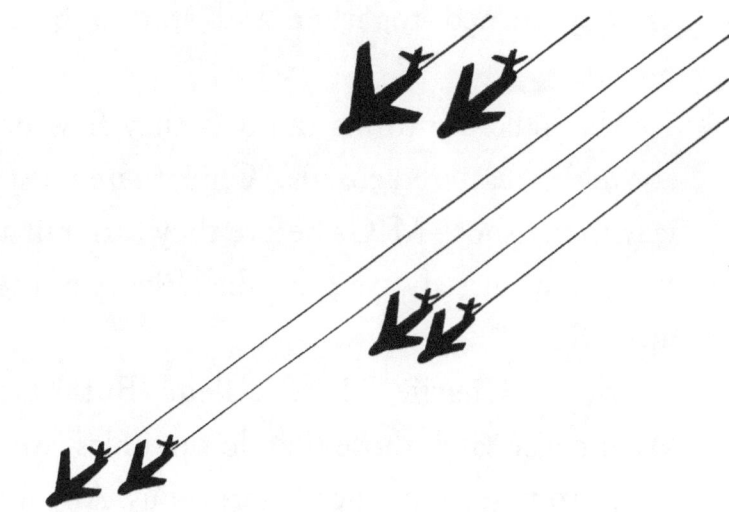

as they turned together and started back toward Suwon.

Mac talked into his radio as they flew homeward above the scattered clouds. "Chip, there must be some way to get those MIGs before they turn tail and run."

"They don't always run, Mac. Plenty of them come up to fight."

"Sure," Charlie Three called. "But Mac's right. We'll never catch those that do run unless we can keep them from getting a head start on us. Any ideas?"

"You've got to see them before they see you."

"Mac saw them."

"That's right. But by the time the rest of us did, it was too late. They were on their way. If only all of us had Mac's eyes."

"If Mac had been leading—" There was a sudden quiet on the radio as Charlie Four seemed to know that he had spoken out of turn. "Sorry, Charlie Leader. I didn't mean—"

Chip's laugh came over the radio. "Forget it, Charlie Four. Maybe I was thinking the same thing. But Mac's not ready to lead yet…not after one combat mission. Just give him time."

It had been a tense moment for Mac. As much as he hoped to graduate from wingman to leader, he knew it would take time. He knew he would have to earn it. And he still hadn't fired a single shot in combat.

To break the silence Mac said, "If we can't catch them, maybe we can get the jump on them some way. Hit them before they see us and have a chance to run away."

"How are you going to do that?" Chip called.

"I don't know," Mac answered. "At least, not yet. But I'm going to try to figure out a way…some way to get the jump on them."

"That's tiger talk, Mac," Charlie Three radioed.

"Maybe," Mac said, smiling to himself. "But that's what we have to do. Get the jump on them…like tigers."

FLIGHT LEADER
CHAPTER 17

DURING THE next few months Mac flew many missions. Winter came with its snow. Bitter, cold winds whipped across the air base. Every one inside huddled around the red-hot stoves. Sometimes clouds lay heavy on the airfield for days at a time, grounding all planes.

But on clear days the Sabres roared into the sky and set out for MIG Alley. More and more MIGs were there waiting for them. Dogfights broke out every day.

"Chip got another one today," Mac cheered in the officers' club after another mission with Charlie Flight. "Eight MIGs came diving down on us from behind. They thought they had us like sitting ducks—"

"But leave it to our wingmen to protect us," one of the other pilots broke in.

"Mac, you called for me to break at just the right time," Chip said, wanting to share his victory. "That

Red pilot was so surprised that he didn't know what to do. I could see it in his eyes as he swept past me. Then it was just a case of cutting back in on his tail and—Bam!"

"Your third red star," Mac said. "Two more and you'll be an ace."

During the days that followed, many MIGs were shot down. But it was not all one-sided. All too often a UN plane failed to return from its mission.

One day Charlie Flight was heading home from MIG Alley when the distress call used by pilots in trouble blasted into their earphones.

"Mayday! Mayday!"

"Someone needs help," Chip radioed. "Anyone see him?"

Mac searched the sky around them. Far to his left, almost out of sight, he saw a thin trail of smoke in the sky.

"Wingman to Charlie Leader. I see him. Nine o'clock. He's on fire!"

"Are you sure, Mac? I don't see anything."

"Nine o'clock," Mac insisted.

"Mayday!" The distress call came again.

"Look, Mac," Chip's voice cut in on the radio. "I still don't see him. But he sure needs help. Take the lead, Mac. Let's see what we can do."

It was strange for Chip to ask Mac to take the lead. But there was little time to think about it. Mac sped ahead. Chip dropped back in the wingman position. Banking left, Mac led Charlie Flight streaking toward the crippled plane.

As they drew nearer, Mac saw that the burning plane was a Thunderjet. It had to be from some other field, as there were no F-84s at Suwon.

Suddenly a figure shot up from the plane's smoking cockpit and then came tumbling down through the air.

"He bailed out," Mac called. "There he goes in his ejection seat!"

Mac watched the pilot kick away from the seat, then pull his ripcord. The parachute snapped open.

"He made it!" Mac shouted. "He made it!"

"We're still in enemy territory," Chip radioed. "We'll give him cover. Protect him until—"

"Chip," Mac called, "you ready to take back the lead now?"

"Stay where you are, Mac. You're doing fine."

They followed the parachute down, circling around it. They kept on the lookout for any enemy plane that might show up and try to take a shot at the flier floating slowly down.

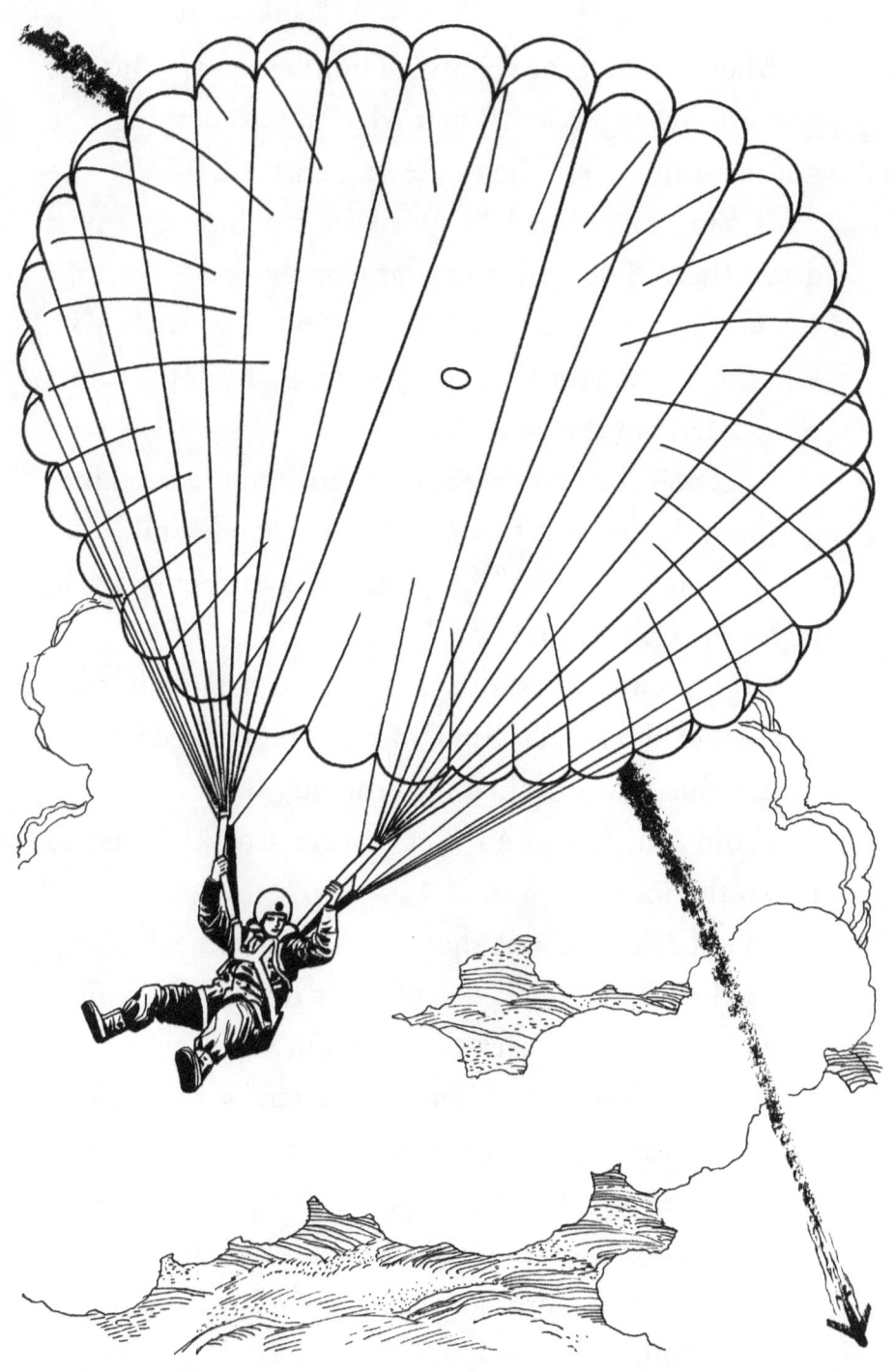

Mac watched the flaming Thunder jet as it hit the ground and exploded. Then Mac saw something else not far from where the plane had crashed.

"Chip," he radioed, "I spotted a machine-gun nest down there. The fellow in that parachute is—"

"Go get it, Mac," Chip cut in. "I'm with you. Charlie Three and Four. Stay with that pilot. Protect him. OK, lead the way, Mac."

Together the two Sabres dived toward the machine-gun nest dug in near the top of a low, wooded hill.

"I see it now, Mac," Chip called. "Let them have it, boy! I'm right behind you."

Mac lined up his sights and pressed the gun button. RAT-TAT-TAT-TAT. Smoking tracers streaked toward the ground and smashed into the target.

From Chip's plane other tracers streaked past to finish the job.

"That takes care of that machine-gun nest," Chip radioed as they pulled out of their dive. "Nice going, Mac. Now let's get back to our flight."

"Charlie Three to Charlie Leader," a voice came into their earphones. "Our boy made it, all right. And there comes a helicopter to pick him up."

Mac banked his plane and looked below. He spotted the helicopter at once. Down low, coming in over the hill.

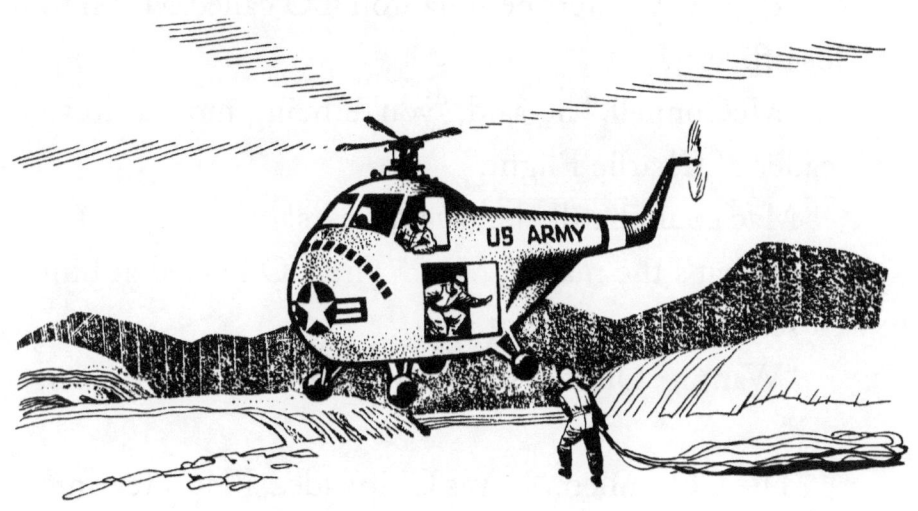

"Oh, those wonderful whirlybirds!" he thought. "Mark up another pilot saved by the Air Rescue Service boys. What a team!"

Charlie Flight circled over the downed pilot until he was picked up safely by the helicopter. The four Sabres stayed around until the whirlybird had crossed back into the friendly territory of South Korea.

"Charlie Flight," Chip radioed, moving back into the lead position. "Let's high-tail it home before we run out of fuel."

Then a strange voice came over the radio. "Charlie Flight, this is the Air Rescue whirlybird. Well done, Charlie Flight. The pilot we just picked up is OK. He sends his thanks."

"No sweat, whirlybird," Chip answered.

A few days later the squadron CO called Mac into his office.

"McConnell," he said, "you're being moved up to leader of Charlie Flight."

Mac could hardly believe his ears.

"What's the matter, Mac?" The CO looked at him closely. "Don't you want it?"

"Want it? Oh, yes, sir. But what about Chip Logan, sir?"

The CO smiled. "It was Chip's idea, Mac. He came to me about it. He said that with your sharp eyes up there in the lead, Charlie Flight would be able to spot and shoot down more MIGs."

"I can see as well from the wingman's position," Mac said.

"Sure. But by the time you've passed the word around until the others find the target, it may be too late to attack. Each second counts."

"Sir," Mac spoke up quickly, "Lieutenant Logan is a fine leader. The best."

"You don't have to tell me, Mac. And don't forget, this is Chip's idea. Chip's eyes are not as good as yours. The worry of being flight leader is telling on him. I think it's best this way. Chip will make a fine wingman for you."

"Oh, I know it, sir," Mac said. "Chip's the best, no matter what position he flies."

"OK, that's all. Tomorrow you take over as leader of Charlie Flight."

That night Chip and Mac had dinner together. Chip said, "It's going to be better this way, Mac. And you'll get your chance to do some shooting now. Plenty of chances. Say, have you worked out any way to get the jump on those MIGs yet? Remember, you were talking about it a while ago."

"I've done a lot of figuring," Mac said. "Even tried working it out on paper. But I won't know for sure if it's any good or not until we try it against a real MIG."

"We'll get our chance," Chip said. "Just wait."

"Chip, that's the big trouble," Mac said. "The waiting. I'm getting tired of it. Real tired. I'm going to get me a MIG—or else!"

FIRST STAR
CHAPTER 18

MAC DIDN'T like the idea, but there was more waiting to come. The weather turned cloudy and bitter cold. There were few good flying days. The pilots huddled around the stoves. They sang together to keep up their restless spirits. They wrote long letters and waited anxiously for word from home.

When the weather was good enough, Charlie Flight went out on missions with Mac flying lead. Several times they saw MIGs, but the Reds did not seem to want a fight. They stayed out of gun range, and the Sabres were not fast enough to catch them.

"The only way we are going to get at those guys," Mac said, "is to get the jump on them."

But the Red pilots always saw the Sabres before they could get the jump.

Then Christmas came. Each barracks had its own Christmas tree cut from the woods nearby. The pilots

fixed up the trees with all the bright things they could find at Suwon Air Base.

"They are not much like our Christmas trees at home," Chip said.

Mac agreed with a nod. "When you come right down to it, there's not much over here that is like home."

Even though the pilots were homesick, they got together for a party. They shared their Christmas boxes from home and tried to have a good time.

It was a good try. They did the best they could. It was a Christmas they would never forget. But at times their eyes clouded up with tears as memories of other Christmases at home came to the men.

In the morning the war was on again.

Three weeks passed, and Mac still had not bagged his first MIG.

One January day in 1953 the sky was full of soft clouds as Mac led Charlie Flight toward MIG Alley. Suddenly they burst out into the bright sunlight. The tops of the clouds spread out beneath them like a great long white rug.

As they drew near to MIG Alley, the other flights of Cobra Squadron spread out to search a wide piece of the sky. There were other planes around and voices on the radio. No need for radio silence now.

"Charlie Leader to Charlie Flight," Mac called. "If we can't climb faster than the MIGs, maybe we can surprise them from below. So I'm going in at a lower altitude. Right on top of the clouds."

"Might work at that, old eagle-eye," Chip radioed back. "Lead on."

Once they were at a lower level, Mac looked up

through the clear plastic of his canopy and into the dark blue sky above. For a long time he saw nothing else but sky.

Then, far to his left and high, he saw a quick flash of sunlight on metal. He looked closer. He saw it now. A MIG! No! Four of them!

Then there was another flash. Another flight of four MIGs! At least, as far as Mac could tell, they were MIGs.

"Charlie Leader to Charlie Flight," Mac called. "Eight bandits at ten o'clock high. See them?"

"Not yet. But lead the way."

"Drop your wing tanks!"

Mac banked to the left and pushed his throttle forward. The three other planes stuck right with him.

"Charlie Three to Charlie Leader. I see them now. Mac, how about me and my wingman going after that second flight, while you and Chip take the first?"

"Roger, Charlie Three. Go to it. But don't get too far away."

As the element broke formation and started after the MIGs, Mac and Chip climbed sharply toward the first flight Mac had sighted.

Like two giant silver bullets, their engines roaring at full power, they streaked up toward the enemy planes.

Mac wanted to tell Chip that he was going to try something new. But there wasn't time for talk. And he knew Chip would follow his lead no matter what.

Suddenly Mac was just where he wanted to be. Below and behind the MIGs so their pilots couldn't see him. The Red planes kept flying straight ahead.

"They haven't seen us yet," Mac thought. "Now to get the jump on them!"

He pushed the throttle wide open. Going at full speed, he cut in front of the leading MIG.

For a brief moment Mac was right in front of the MIG's guns. By the time the surprised Red pilot saw him, it was too late to pull the trigger.

Mac cut to the left in a screaming turn. The MIG pilot banked and started after him. But when the MIG got halfway into the turn, Mac switched controls and cut back sharply into the Commie plane.

The MIG flashed into his gun sight. Mac pressed the gun button.

RAT-TAT-TAT-TAT-TAT-TAT-TAT-TAT—

The Sabre bucked as the smoking bullets streaked ahead like bees with their tails on fire. Some of them slammed into the MIG. The plane wobbled a bit but kept on flying. Mac cut in from behind.

"Nice going, Mac!" Chip's excited voice shouted over the radio. "You slowed him down. But watch out! He's not finished yet!"

"That goes for me, too." Mac called, starting to bank the other way. "Keep an eye on those other MIGs, Chip."

"I'm watching, Mac. But they don't seem to want a fight. Not after the way you got the jump on them."

Mac didn't answer. He was too busy trying to get the MIG back in his sights. The Red was a good pilot. He rolled and dived, trying to shake Mac off. But Mac's first bullets had slowed him down. When the MIG rolled and dived, Mac followed. Once again he had the MIG lined up in his sights.

Mac pressed the gun button once more and held it. More bullets burst from the Sabre's nose. They streaked through the sky, many of them slamming into the MIG.

Black smoke poured from the enemy plane. Then a red burst of flame shot into the sky as the MIG exploded. Mac banked sharply out of the way of the flying pieces.

"You got him," Chip yelled over the radio. "Your first MIG! You're a tiger for sure now!"

A strange feeling swept over Mac. Shooting down his first MIG was something he had thought about for months. Now he felt the victory deeply. This one MIG would no longer hunt and shoot down his buddies. This one MIG would no longer fight against free people.

"Charlie Two to Charlie Leader," Chip's voice came again. "Can you hear me, Mac? Come in."

Mac pressed his mike button. "Sorry, Chip," he said. "I hear you. But I was thinking."

"Sure you were, pal. I remember my first MIG. But you did a beautiful job of flying, Mac. Never saw anything like it before. Give out, boy. What gave you the idea?"

"Oh, that," Mac said, watching the other MIGs head across the Yalu. "Well, it's really kind of simple,

Chip. But I guess I worked it out on paper a hundred times. As you know, a MIG can't bank as sharply as a Sabre."

"That's right. What's that got to do with it?"

"Well, first you have to surprise the MIG pilot before he sees you and starts to run away. Then you cut across in front of him. When he starts to follow, thinking you're a sitting duck, you bank sharply into him from the side. When he tries to bank with you, he starts to wobble and loses speed. You're back in on his tail before he knows it. You slow him down with your first burst. Maybe you even get him. But if he's still flying and tries to get away, you come in sharply from the other side and give him another burst."

"Man alive!" Chip cried. "I see it now. You get him from both directions. Fake to the left, then hit him from the right. Then fake again and hit him from the left side. Mac, it sounds like the old one-two. Sure as shooting, it sounds like the old one-two punch that fighters use!"

Mac smiled to himself. He was thinking of his fight years ago with a fellow named Al Kroger. Way back in basic training. Years and years ago!

The old one-two. It had been good then…down on the ground.

It was still good…high in the sky!

JET ACE
CHAPTER 19

WITH MAC in the lead, Charlie Flight soon headed back to Suwon. The journey home was a good one.

Later, Steve was helping Mac out of his harness and parachute when Chip ran over and climbed up on the wing. He slapped Mac on the back.

"You're in there with the big boys now, Mac!" he shouted. "Your first MIG."

"Thanks to you, Chip."

"You almost lost me a couple of times," Chip said. "Boy, the way you were twisting your Sabre around!"

"It worked, though," Mac said. "And with you as my wingman I didn't have to worry about one of those other MIGs shooting me down from behind. We'll go after them now, Chip?"

"Right," Chip agreed. "We'll cut them up with the old one-two."

That night at the officers' club the pilots who had

shot down MIGs welcomed Mac into the group. "Just four more to go and you will be an ace."

There were already a few aces at Suwon—men who had shot down five or more MIGs. There were others up at Kimpo. Among them was Pete, the fellow Mac had met on the plane coming from Japan to Korea.

"Looks like I'll have to buy Pete a dinner," Mac said, thinking once again of their friendly bet.

But it didn't really matter to Mac, or any of the others, how many MIGs each shot down. The thing that was important was to end the war. If shooting down MIGs was one way to help—and it surely was—then each would shoot down as many as he could.

"If it takes as long to get the next four MIGs as it did to get the first one," Mac said, "I'll be an old man before I'm an ace."

In the days that followed, many more air battles took place. More and more Red planes came down along MIG Alley looking for a fight. And the UN planes were always there to give it to them. Mac shot down his second MIG in much the same way as he had bagged his first.

"It's the old one-two," Chip told the other pilots and explained how Mac did it.

Some of the others tried using the one-two, but they had less luck with it than Mac.

"It's those eagle eyes of his," Steve Davis said when Mac shot down his third MIG. Steve was painting a third red star on the side of Mac's Sabre. "He sees them and goes after them before the MIGs have a chance to run away."

But during the early spring of 1953 the MIGs began to run away less and less. UN planes were bombing the dams, railroads, and supply centers all over North Korea. Swarms of UN bombers flew both day and night missions. Soon the Communists were short of power supply, short of bullets, and short of most other things needed to fight a war.

Now the Commies had to fight back in the air or be bombed out.

So the MIGs began coming down across the Yalu in greater numbers. The Sabres and Thunderjets flew up to meet them over MIG Alley. Most of the time there were about ten MIGs to every UN plane. But the UN pilots were shooting down nearly ten MIGs to every one of their own planes lost in battle.

"Those Commies aren't very good shots, are they?" Mac said to Chip on the day he shot down his fourth MIG.

"Well, don't count on it," Chip warned. "Once today I thought one of those Reds had you dead center in his sights."

"He didn't know what a great wingman you are, pal," Mac said. "You chased him off before he could touch me."

"That's why I'm back there, Mac. Just the same, it doesn't always work. The main thing is for you not to get careless. I sure don't want anything to happen to you."

"How can they beat a team like us?"

"Easy," Chip said. "Just be careless, or take one chance too many!"

A couple days later Steve was waiting on the flight line when Mac and Chip came out to their planes.

"Steve, be sure Mac's guns are loaded," Chip kidded. "He's going to become an ace today. Aren't you, Mac?"

"We might make it if we run into some MIGs," Mac answered. "But why don't you fly the lead today. Chip?"

"No, thanks, Mac, I'm used to being your wingman now. I like it. We work better that way."

Mac climbed into his plane. Steve helped him put on his parachute and shoulder harness straps. He looked closely at Mac.

"What's the matter, Steve? What's on your mind?"

"Oh, it's really nothing, Mac."

"Go on. Tell me, pal."

"It's this ace business, Mac. We all want you to become an ace. You've earned it."

"Not yet. I still have one more MIG to go."

"Sure, I know, Mac. And you'll get it. But don't try to hurry it. You may get careless. You may take too many chances."

There it was again, Mac thought. Why was everyone talking about getting careless, or taking too many chances? Sure, he had taken some chances. You had to in order to make the old one-two work.

"Cheer up, Steve," he said. "Being an ace isn't everything. I know that. But, remember, if I become an ace you have had plenty to do with it. A pilot is no better than his crew chief, you know. I can't shoot down MIGs unless my plane is in top shape. And you sure have kept it that way, pal. So when and if I become an ace, you will, too."

"OK, Mac, that's fine with me," Steve said. "But take your time. If you get shot down we will never make it."

"Thanks. I needed a little talking to today. When a fellow shoots down four MIGs he can't wait to go after number five."

Soon Cobra Squadron flew north toward the Yalu. As they neared the river, they saw a big dogfight ahead. A swarm of MIGs and several Sabres from another

squadron were chasing one another through the sky. A plane fell twisting and spinning, trailing smoke and flame.

"Cobra Leader to all Cobra flights," the squadron commander's voice came over the air. "This is a big one. Our boys need some help. Pick your targets. Every flight for itself."

"Charlie Leader to Charlie Flight," Mac called. "Let's go after that bunch on the left."

"We're with you, Mac."

Charlie Flight broke away from the squadron. The flight kept in tight formation, climbing steeply toward the air battle high and to the left.

Mac could tell as they closed in that he would not

be able to use the old one-two today. There was little chance of getting the jump on any MIG. No chance for surprise. Everyone saw everyone else.

This would be straight fighting. Every element or every flight would be on its own.

"Wingman to Charlie One," Chip called suddenly over his radio. "Watch out, Mac! There's a bandit diving down on you from behind!"

"How far back, Chip?"

"A half mile. And closing fast, Mac."

"Keep your eye on him, Chip. He doesn't know we see him. Let him come at me. Tell me when to break. But wait until the very last second. Wait until you think he's about ready to fire."

"Mac, you're crazy! How do I know when he's going to fire?"

"Guess, Chip. Guess."

"You won't last a—"

"I have an idea. No time to explain."

Mac smiled to himself. Chip had a good reason to think he was crazy. Mac was setting himself up as a sitting duck for the MIG!

The thought made Mac shiver. But he kept flying straight ahead as if he had no idea that the MIG was diving down on him from behind. He could almost feel the Communist bullets slamming into him.

But so far it was only in his mind. How soon would it be real? Why wasn't Chip calling for him to break? If he waited one second too long—

Then Chip's voice shouted over the radio, "Get ready to break to the right, Mac! Ready! Break!"

Mac rolled his Sabre sharply to the right. The force of the quick turn jammed him deep into his seat.

The MIG went whistling past, bullets barely missing Mac's plane. But they did miss.

He banked to the left and cut toward the MIG. Before the Red pilot knew what had happened, Mac gave him a long burst with his machine guns.

A piece of the MIG's wing flew off. Then the Red plane started to burn. Suddenly the pilot bailed out in his ejection seat.

Mac whizzed past close enough to almost see the Commie's face as he tumbled end over end through the air. His parachute hadn't opened yet.

Then the Red pilot dropped out of sight. The MIG plane dived on down to crash in a big burst of orange flame.

"Mac, you did it!" Chip cried. "Number five!"

"That's right," Mac thought. "Number five."

"You're an ace, Mac!" Chip was calling. "You're an ace! Hey, Mac, do you hear me?"

"I hear you, Chip."

The sight of the MIG pilot tumbling through the air was still in his mind.... He wondered if the man's parachute ever opened.

SPECIAL MISSION
CHAPTER 20

THERE WERE five red stars on Mac's Sabre. Then there were six. A few days later, seven.

And on Mac's shoulders were two silver bars where before there had been one. He was now a captain.

Captain Joseph McConnell, Jr., United States Air Force. Mac was proud of that. Very proud.

"You've earned it," Chip said. "Everyone in Korea is talking about Joe McConnell and his seven MIGs."

"You wouldn't kid me, would you?" Mac asked. "My friend Pete up in Kimpo has more than that."

Chip smiled. "He has got more right now, Mac. But keep up the way you've been going and Pete will be the one to buy the dinners. You're a roaring tiger, boy!"

"You've been doing plenty of roaring yourself," Mac said. "Don't forget, you got your fourth the other day. You'll be an ace soon. The war isn't over yet."

In fact, during the next days the fighting got even

worse. It was late spring. The snow was gone. The dark storm clouds moved on. The sun came out to warm the land.

It was the best flying weather Mac had seen since coming to Korea. The blazing air battles along MIG Alley grew hotter each day.

One morning Chip wasn't feeling well. Nothing serious. But a good fighter pilot knew better than to fly when he wasn't in the best of health.

Mac flew the day's mission with another wingman. They sighted some MIGs and gave chase. But they weren't able to catch the Red planes. After searching a while longer for some other MIGs, Charlie Flight turned back for Suwon.

The next morning Chip was sitting up in his bunk. Mac asked him, "How are you feeling?"

"Great."

"You sure don't look it."

"You're no Miss America yourself, Mac."

They laughed. But Chip had to say that he still didn't feel very well.

"Don't worry about me, Mac," he said. "Go have fun. This is your day of rest."

"Boy, and I can use it. Those MIGs have been giving us plenty of trouble. I missed you yesterday, Chip. The other fellow was all right. But you're the best wingman a guy ever had."

Just then a young sergeant came to the door. "Lieutenant Logan?" he asked.

"I'm Lieutenant Logan," Chip answered. "What's up?"

"The CO wants you to fly a special mission today, sir."

"What about Captain McConnell?"

"He didn't say anything about Captain McConnell, sir."

Chip started to get up.

"Hey, Chip," said Mac. "You can't fly today. Not the way you feel. Hey, didn't you report yesterday that you were sick?"

"Well, I thought I'd be all right today."

"You're not," Mac said. "Not well enough to fly, that's for sure." Then Mac turned to the sergeant. "Tell the CO I'll be right over."

"Yes, sir, Captain McConnell." The sergeant saluted and left.

"Mac, you can't do it," Chip said. "You were out on two missions yesterday. This is your day to rest. That's why the CO sent for me."

"There'll be plenty of time to rest after the war. Now, stay in bed. I'll see you later."

Mac hurried to the CO's office. "Lieutenant Logan is a little under the weather. I'll carry out any orders for him. What's up, sir?"

"One of our Sabres ran out of fuel coming back from MIG Alley. He went down in enemy territory.

About a hundred miles north and west of here. The other planes in his flight were low on fuel, too. They had to leave him."

"What about the pilot?" Mac asked quickly.

"One of the men in the flight thought he saw a parachute open, but he wasn't sure. The plane might have gone down in the Yellow Sea. The pilot called Mayday. That's the last anyone heard. A helicopter is out looking for him. It needs protection. I was going to have Chip pick a wingman and fly cover for the whirlybird."

"Simple enough," Mac said with a smile. "An old man's mission. I'd still like to go, sir."

"Well, all right, Mac. You win. Get over to the briefing room and see whom you can get for your wingman. Most of the flights have already gone out. I'm not sure just how many wingmen are left. They will have a list over there. Good luck on the mission."

"No sweat, sir," Mac said.

Mac hurried to the barracks to get his flying suit. Then he went to the briefing room. All the wingmen he knew were out on missions. Mac let the officer pick a wingman for him.

"He's a new kid," the officer told Mac. "Just finished his practice missions."

"Is he ready for combat?"

"He's ready. A little green, but ready."

In a couple of minutes the two planes were flying north. Mac noticed the wingman was flying too far behind him. "A new kid," Mac said to himself. "Well, I was new at this stuff not so long ago, too."

Mac looked below. He had not yet spotted the helicopter. Still, he figured it should be showing up most any minute, now that they were nearing enemy territory.

Mac radioed to his wingman. "Close in, fellow. You're hanging back too far. You're like a sitting duck. Me, too, for that matter."

The distance between the two planes stayed almost the same. "Wingman to Leader," the call came in. "I—I'm not getting full power from my engine, and—"

"Watch out!" Mac cut in on the radio. As he looked back toward his wingman a flash of sun on metal caught his eye. "There's a MIG on your tail. Break left. Break left!"

The wingman banked sharply. But the MIG was already on top of him, pouring hot bullets into the crippled Sabre.

"I—I'm hit!" the call came. "Sorry, McConnell, I—I—"

The Sabre exploded.

Mac shouted with rage and rolled his plane in be-

hind the MIG as it tried to pull out of its screaming dive.

The Red plane climbed, starting into a loop, as the pilot tried to get around behind Mac. But Mac stuck right with him, climbed with him, rolled with him.

Now the MIG went into a dive. Mac stuck right with it as the two planes roared toward the ground.

Then Mac got the MIG in his sights.

RAT-TAT-TAT-TAT-TAT-TAT-TAT-TAT—

Bullets smashed into the enemy plane. The MIG wobbled out of control and started to spin. Mac followed it down—down—down, his guns blazing.

At the last moment he pulled the Sabre out of its dive. The MIG kept spinning until it crashed into a hill and exploded.

Mac gave no thought to the fact that he had shot down another MIG—number eight. He was sad and full of rage for having lost his wingman, a boy he hardly knew. Even though Mac had seen death before, it was never easy to look upon.

"I had better get out of here," he thought. "This is no place for a lone plane. Besides, who knows where that whirlybird is by now? And I'm getting low on fuel."

He turned out over the Yellow Sea, heading south. Heading back for K-13, Suwon.

He had just finished making his turn when from out of nowhere bullets came smashing into his Sabre!

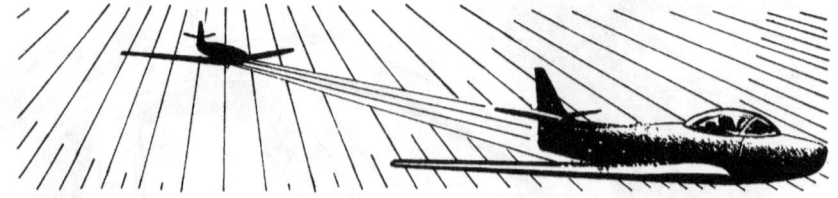

BAIL OUT
CHAPTER 21

Mac never did know where the MIG had come from, out of the sky. Probably it had come diving down out of the sun's glare so that he couldn't see it. That was an old trick, and a good one. No matter where or how, the MIG had done its job well.

Mac jammed hard on the stick and rudder, trying to get out of the way. But the bullets kept coming. They smashed into his wings, leaving great holes. They slammed into the body of the Sabre, tearing away pieces of metal. Some crashed into the cockpit, wrecking instruments. The bullets left little white lines spreading out from holes in the plastic canopy. But, by some chance, the bullets missed him!

The Red MIG swept on past, its guns still blazing.

"That MIG will get me on his next pass," Mac told himself. "He'll turn around and come back to finish me off. And I can't fight back. I can't do a thing to stop him."

But the MIG didn't turn around. It kept right on going north toward the Yalu.

Mac took a deep breath and grinned. "He thinks he got me. Or maybe he's running low on fuel, too, and has to return to his base."

What a break. And right now Mac needed all the breaks he could get.

The Sabre was dropping fast. To make matters worse, Mac was still far behind enemy lines.

He looked around. Jet fuel was pouring from the bullet holes in his wings. Instruments had been smashed. The controls worked hard.

"I don't know what more could go wrong," he said to himself. "Unless I was on fire! Then it would be a quick end for sure!"

He looked at his altimeter. "How high?" he wondered. "How high?" But the altimeter had been wrecked by the bullets crashing into the cockpit.

He glanced over the side of the plane. Below was the Yellow Sea with its cold, angry waters. Close—much too close.

"I have to make it home," Mac told himself. "I have to get this plane back to Suwon."

Mac was wondering what to do when a voice came over his radio earphones. "Blue Dog to crippled Sabre. What's your trouble?"

Mac turned to see an F-84 Thunder jet pulling up alongside his left wingtip.

"Your plane's all shot up, tiger," the Thunderjet pilot called. "What about you?"

"I'm all right, Blue Dog," Mac answered, glad to find that his radio hadn't been hit.

"Hey, that MIG really poured it on to you, boy. You can't get home in your Sabre."

"I still have a wing and a prayer."

"All you have is a prayer, buddy. And you're losing altitude fast. Better bail out."

Bail out? Mac hadn't even thought of that. All he had been thinking about was trying to save his plane.

His fingers searched for the trigger of the ejection seat. But he didn't want to bail out. Not if there was any chance at all to save his Sabre.

"How high am I?" he asked.

"Three thousand feet," the voice came back. "What's the matter? Is your altimeter shot up?"

"Yes."

"Look, don't chance it, buddy," the Thunderjet pilot called. "Bail out! I'll radio your position back to your base. Somebody will try to pick you up. I'll stick around as long as I can. But call Mayday and bail out. Now!"

Mac looked to the south. Far in the distance was South Korea...Suwon Air Base...home!

A long way off. And the Sabre was dropping faster than ever.

"Bail out!" the Thunderjet pilot called again. "You don't stand a chance of flying that plane back to your base."

Mac looked down at the Yellow Sea. He saw the water very close beneath him, and a shiver went through him. It took time to bail out! Time to kick away from the ejection seat once he was tumbling through the air. It took time for his parachute to open after pulling the ripcord. And during all that time he would be falling—falling.

If he didn't bail out high enough his parachute wouldn't open in time. It had happened to others. They hadn't lived to tell about it.

Mac was sure now that there was no chance to save his plane. He flipped a switch. "Mayday," he called over the radio. "Mayday."

Mac pulled a handle and the plastic canopy over his head flew off. The wind burst into the cockpit, smashing him into the seat. He braced himself and squeezed the ejection seat trigger.

At once the seat exploded and shot him straight up into the air. The force knocked the breath out of him. Once he was out of the plane the wind smashed against him harder than ever. It tore off his helmet and oxygen mask. Then he began spinning and tumbling through the air.

"Quick!" he thought. "Get rid of the seat!"

He slipped out of the strap and kicked with all his might against the metal rests of the seat. It fell away. He was free. Falling fast—falling!

He reached for the ring on his parachute harness. He jerked it hard! The ripcord came loose in his hand. As he kept tumbling, the sight of the water flashed close—close—closer.

The parachute still had not opened. Had he waited

too long? Mac braced himself. He didn't know why. It would do him no good if the parachute didn't open.

Then, suddenly, there was a loud pop. With a jerk the giant parachute opened. Like a great cloud it spread out above him. A moment later he hit the water!

BRAVE MEN AND BULLETS
CHAPTER 22

HELD UP by his Mae West, Mac lay in the bitter cold water of the Yellow Sea. Already the cold was chilling him to the bone.

He could see the land—enemy land. And he was floating in enemy water. He looked up and saw planes flying toward him in the distance. He counted eight, coming from different directions. Were they enemy planes? If so, that one Thunderjet overhead couldn't keep them away. Were they coming to shoot him as he floated helpless in the water? Oh, no, that was no way for a fighter pilot to die!

As the planes came closer he let out a yell, "Sabres! Thunderjets!"

He waved and shouted as the planes started around him. "They all heard me call Mayday, and came whizzing over here to protect me from any MIGs that might be around. What a bunch of guys!"

He waved some more to let them know he was still alive. They wobbled their wings in answer.

"But what now?" Mac asked himself. "How am I going to get out of here? I'm so cold now that I don't think I can take it much longer. A whirlybird would be taking a big chance coming this far into enemy territory to try to save me. I can't expect them to do that."

But it was only a few minutes later when he heard the strange sound of a helicopter. Then he saw it coming in low over the water toward him. As it came closer he could make out the letters on its side…US Air Force—Air Rescue Service.

"Oh, you beautiful, beautiful whirlybird!" Mac shouted.

The helicopter came down low to hang still in the air just over his head.

A sergeant looking out the open door of the helicopter grinned down at Mac. Quickly he lowered a wire with a harness on the end. Mac wrapped the straps around his shoulders and snapped them tight.

Then he was lifted out of the water and up—up to the helicopter. Strong hands reached out and pulled him inside. Mac was wet and shivering with the cold, but he was happy to have been rescued.

"Been having fun, Captain?" the whirlybird's sergeant asked as he put a warm cover around Mac.

"You might call it that," Mac answered with a laugh. "But I've had more fun at other times."

"Well, you're safe now, sir. Just leave it to the Air Rescue Service to see that you sizzling jet boys get back home safe and sound."

"Sergeant, you are so right. You fellows are the greatest. Many thanks."

"All part of the day's work, sir," the sergeant said. But his eyes were shining proudly.

Glancing out the window, Mac saw the jets turn and fly south. They had done their job of protecting him, and they were heading home.

"How soon can you get me back to Suwon, Sergeant?" Mac asked. "I have another mission to fly this afternoon."

"Are you kidding me, sir? You've done enough flying for one day."

An hour later Mac was back at Suwon. But there was no more flying for him that day.

But the next day Mac was ready to fly again. There was another Sabre waiting for him on the flight line. As always, Steve Davis stood beside the plane waiting for him.

"Sorry to hear about your wingman yesterday, Mac," the friendly crew chief said. "And, boy, am I ever glad to see you back safe. We've been losing too many

Publisher's note: This drawing is based on a photo of the rescue.

pilots—ones that don't get back. Don't let it happen to you, Mac."

"I won't, Steve…not if I can help it."

Then Mac noticed the angry look on his crew chief's face. "What's the matter, Steve?"

"The pilot of that Thunderjet who helped you yesterday called here to see how you made out," Steve answered. "He told the CO he had asked you to bail out. Asked you again and again. But he said you stayed with the plane until—until it was almost too late to make it."

"Oh, it wasn't that bad," Mac argued. But he well knew that he had bailed out just in time. "We need all the planes we have to beat those Reds. We can't lose even one plane if there's any way to save it."

"Well, staying with a plane until it crashes doesn't save the plane or the pilot. Be more careful after this, Mac. Please." His anger was gone.

"Sure, Steve. Sure. Now let's get our Sabre fired up and into the air."

That day, and for the next couple of weeks, Mac flew with a new wingman. Chip had been sicker than he had thought, and had been kept in the base hospital.

During that time Charlie Flight shot down three more MIGs. Mac got one of them—number nine for him.

Word had come down from Kimpo that his friend Pete was ahead of him on MIG kills. Eleven of them to date. The friendly race between Mac and Pete had become the talk of the air bases all over South Korea. Back in the United States they talked about it too.

When Chip reported back for duty a few days later he was well and rested. "Sorry to be gone so long, Mac," he said. "But I hear you fellows did all right. How was your new wingman?"

"He was all right. But I'm glad you're back, Chip. I'd rather fly with you than anyone else. We know each other's every move. We almost know what the other is thinking."

"You get that way when you've flown together as much as we have," Chip said.

Toward the end of the week the whole squadron got into a big dogfight south of the Yalu. Eleven MIGs were shot down. Mac got one of them.

"That's ten, Mac," called Chip.

"I saw it crash, Mac," Charlie Three radioed. "You're a double-ace, fellow! That's going some!"

That night there was a big time in the officers' club. Double-aces were few and far between.

During the coming days the Communists seemed to be making their last big stand. They started sending all the planes they could into the sky along MIG Alley.

But the UN jets shot them down almost as fast as they were sent up.

Within a few days Mac shot down three more MIGs...eleven, twelve, and thirteen. Chip got two of his own, breaking off and chasing planes that tried to get in behind Mac for a shot. Chip was now an ace—with an extra MIG.

For a few days Mac was tied with Pete. Then word came down from Kimpo that Pete had shot down another enemy plane. Number fourteen.

"Boy," Mac laughed to himself, "Pete is sure dead set on my buying him a dinner."

Then one spring day in the middle of May Mac's flight went out on a morning mission. When they reached MIG Alley they found the sky swarming with planes, mostly MIGs. Soon another squadron of UN fighters joined the battle. More than fifty planes were spread out all over the sky.

"Each element break off and pick your own MIG," the Cobra Squadron commander called. "No point in trying to stick close together in this dogfight."

"Charlie Leader to wingman," Mac called. "Let's go get them, Chip!"

"I'm right with you, Mac."

Mac picked out a group of four MIGs high and far

to his right. He climbed toward them, keeping to one side, hoping they wouldn't see him or Chip.

They didn't. Mac got the first one with the old one-two. Fourteen MIGs! The pilot bailed out. He tumbled through the air, kicking free from his ejection seat.

Mac knew just how the Commie pilot must have felt. The memory of his own bail-out was still in his mind.

"Get ready to break, Mac!" Chip's warning shout over the radio jerked him out of his thoughts. "Ready to break to the left! There's a MIG coming in on your tail!"

Mac could tell from the sound of Chip's voice how close the MIG was. Much the same thing had happened many times before.

"Call when, Chip!"

There was a short pause.

"Break, Mac! Now!"

Mac banked sharply to the left. As the Red plane sped past, Mac rolled his Sabre. The Red plane crossed through his sights. Mac let him have a quick burst. He saw the bullets cut a line of dark holes along the side of the MIG.

The Communist plane fell in flames.

"Number fifteen, Mac!" Chip called excitedly. "Know what that means? You're a triple-ace, Mac. The only triple-ace in the whole Korean War! The only triple jet ace in the whole wide world!"

That same afternoon several flights from Cobra Squadron went out again. Charlie Flight was one of them. And Mac shot down another MIG...his third in one day. Number sixteen.

That night the other pilots gave Mac the biggest party that Suwon Air Base had seen since the Korean War began.

In the morning the commanding officer of the base called Mac into his office. "McConnell," he said, "I'm afraid you're through in Korea."

"Through? I don't understand, sir," Mac said, wondering what the CO meant.

"You've already flown well over a hundred missions," the CO went on. "That's more than we ask of any man, Captain."

"I want to keep flying, sir."

"You have shot down sixteen MIGs," the CO reminded. "More than anyone else in this whole war. Even your friend Pete up at Kimpo."

"But there are still MIGs in the sky, sir. And the war isn't over."

"It soon will be, Mac. The Commies are on the run. Thanks to guys like you."

"They're good at running, sir," Mac said, smiling.

"Sixteen of them should have run faster," the CO said. "But enough of that. The fighting's over for you, Mac. We're sending you back to the United States."

"But, sir, why?"

The commanding officer smiled. "I'd let you stay if I could, Mac. But the orders come from higher up. Pete is being sent home, too. You boys have more fighting experience than anyone else around here. They want both of you to use that experience to teach young new pilots back home."

That part of it sounded all right to Mac. But there was just one thing—

"Sir," he said, "can't I use that same experience right here to help finish off the war...to help win lasting freedom for the South Koreans?"

"I'm afraid not," the CO said. He looked closely at Mac. "But, Captain, on that matter of winning freedom. I wouldn't worry too much about that. You already have won a big share of freedom...for the Koreans—and for all the world."

LAST FLIGHT
CHAPTER 23

THERE WAS little time for good-bys. But Mac and Chip and Steve had one long last talk about the things they had done together, and the things they wanted to do when the war was over.

"I'm going to be a school teacher," Chip said.

"You'll make a good one," Steve said. "But I think I'll stick to the Air Force. Oh, maybe one of these days some airline company will start flying jets and I'll get a job with them. It's coming. Mark my words. And maybe I can fit into the picture someplace."

"Sure you will," Mac said. "You're a great fellow with jets, Steve."

"Thanks. What are you going to do, Mac? As if I had to ask." Steve laughed.

"I can guess that one, too," Chip added, smiling. "You love flying, don't you, Mac?"

"For me there's nothing else. Nothing else."

Early one morning Mac was on his way across the ocean toward the United States—home. Pete was on the plane, too. They talked of all the things that had happened since they had last seen each other.

"And when we get back to the States," Pete said, "I'll buy you the biggest dinner you ever put under your belt, Mac. You earned it."

"No more than you, Pete. I was lucky, that's all. Tell you what, I'll buy the second helpings."

They laughed. Soon the talking ended and they were deep in their own thoughts.

A few hours later the plane landed on an island air base to fill up with gas. Then it took off again. Before long the hum of the transport's engines put Mac to sleep. He didn't open his eyes again until the plane landed. And this time he was home...the United States...America...wonderful, wonderful America!

The first few weeks back in the United States were busy ones for Mac. Exciting ones, too. He flew to Washington, D.C. He was taken to see the President, a day which he was not to forget.

There were other big days for Mac. Many medals were given to him. He was called the world's greatest jet ace, triple jet ace, in fact.

But there was something much more important to Mac than all the names and all the honors.

"I want to fly," he kept saying to his new commanding officer. "If I was sent back here to teach new pilots, I better start teaching them. The Air Force can use more pilots in Korea."

His new CO understood how Mac felt about flying. So he sent Mac out West to teach new young pilots about flying the latest jets.

Two months later in July, 1953, the war in Korea ended. Because of help from the United Nations, the South Koreans were still a free people.

"There won't be such a hurry for new pilots now, Mac," his CO told him. "Oh, we'll need them. We'll always need new pilots. But the big rush is over for now. You take it easy for a while. Rest up. You've earned it."

But Mac didn't know what it was to take it easy. He had always worked hard for everything. It was the only way he knew. And he liked it. He could not sit still.

So he kept flying in the Air Force. New models of the Sabre were being made. They were even better than the F-86s Mac had flown in Korea. They were full of new instruments which made flying easier. Mac tried them out.

"With these new instruments," he told the young pilots, "you don't even have to see an enemy plane to shoot it down. The instruments see it for you. They can even tell when to fire the guns—and fire them for you!"

"If there is ever another war," one of the pilots said, "they may not even need a pilot in the plane. Let the instruments do everything. So what am I doing here learning to be a pilot?"

Mac smiled. "Don't worry. The instruments aren't that good yet. They still make mistakes. No, an airplane still needs a man at the controls. A good man. And it will be that way for a long time to come."

So he kept right on teaching new pilots. Soon it was the middle of 1954. One hot day out on the desert base where Mac was on duty an Air Force colonel came to see him.

"Captain McConnell," the colonel said, "this is a secret matter. Top secret. We have a new model of the Sabre that has to be tested. We think it will be the fastest thing in the sky."

"You think it will be?" Mac asked. "Don't you know, sir?"

"No. Not yet. No one has flown it to find out for sure. Mac, you're the best Sabre jet pilot around, so we thought you might like to try it."

Mac jumped to his feet. "Would I!" he cried. "Where is it?"

The colonel smiled. "Well, it's not parked outside, Mac. But it's not far from here. It's up at Edwards Air Force Base."

Mac knew about the Edwards Base. That is, he knew as much as anyone on the outside knew about the country's top secret test base. Edwards was where all the new model planes were tested before being sent to the Air Force.

"You want me to be a test pilot?" Mac asked.

"That's it, Captain," the colonel answered. "If you want to try it."

"I'll say I want to try it!"

In the weeks that passed, Mac flew the new Sabre jet many times. He started out slowly. On each flight he tried something new. He tested the new instruments one by one. Each time he flew he opened the throttle a little wider—went a little faster.

"She handles like a pilot's dream plane," he reported to the officer at the base. "She's fast. She climbs like a yo-yo. Tomorrow I hope they will let me open her up wide and see what she can really do!"

And in the morning Mac took off once again from the long runway at Edwards. He pointed the plane steeply into the sky and called the control tower to talk to the officers there.

"Everything is fine up here," Mac reported to them. "How about making a high speed run?"

"Permission granted," the tower operator answered. "Keep us posted."

He took a deep breath. "Here goes!" he called. He pushed the throttle full ahead.

The Sabre went screaming through the sky.

Mac checked the instruments and the controls in the cockpit with great care. Everything was working fine.

Faster than the speed of sound. Everything was going great. Mac had never flown such a plane!

Then, in a flash, and without warning, something went wrong!

The Sabre began to shake as though it would fall to pieces. It nosed over and Mac was sure that at any moment it might go into a dive. He pulled back on the throttle and fought with the controls. At first they wouldn't move. Finally through muscle power alone he was able to move them enough to get the plane back in level flight.

Yet, things were not right—not right at all! The plane was touchy. It was losing altitude.

He was down low already, but not too low to bail out. And the plane shook like a rag in a dog's mouth.

"What's the matter up there, Mac?"

Mac knew that he was close enough now for them to see him from the control tower. Every one in the tower knew he was in trouble. They could tell by the way the plane was bouncing and bucking through the sky.

"The controls stuck," Mac answered quickly. "Bad shaking in wing and tail, and—"

"Bail out, Mac!" a voice shouted into his earphones. "You're getting low!"

"I'll try—I'll try to bring her in," Mac said, trying to keep his voice steady.

This was a good plane, a great plane. It was valuable to the safety of the country, perhaps to the safety of the world. If he bailed out, no one would ever know what had gone wrong.

And, to Mac, it was important that they know so they could fix it. It was important to know in order to keep this from happening when someone else was flying the same kind of plane.

More than anything else, Mac wanted to bring that plane in safely. But it still bucked and shook badly. It was losing altitude fast.

"Bail out, Mac!" the shout came again. "That's an order! Do you hear? Bail out!"

There was no answer.

Out on the desert, on the far side of a low hill, there was a flash of flame. A cloud of black smoke burst into the air.

A few seconds later the sound of the crash reached the control tower.

August 25, 1954, Captain Joseph McConnell, Jr., United States Air Force, was killed testing a late model Sabre jet, F-86H. Mac, the triple jet ace, had gone on his last flight.

Once they had said that Mac was too old to fly. How wrong they had been. But one thing was sure. At thirty-two he was too young to die. In the few short years he wore his pilot wings he had been a flying tiger. Always he had fought hard for what he believed in—an end to wars—freedom for all people.

www.ingramcontent.com/pod-product-compliance
Lightning Source LLC
LaVergne TN
LVHW041703060526
838201LV00043B/549